...UNDATION PUBLICATION

שירות ותשבחות

THE
NCSY BENCHER

A BOOK OF PRAYER
AND SONG

Edited and translated by
David Olivestone

National Conference of Synagogue Youth
Union of Orthodox Jewish Congregations of America

Revised Edition, 1993.
Forty-ninth printing, 2012.

Copyright © 1982, 1983, 1993 by the Orthodox Union.

English translations copyright © 1982, 1993 by David Olivestone.

Published by OU/NCSY Publications,
Orthodox Union, Eleven Broadway, New York, NY 10004.
212.563.4000 • www.ou.org.

Distributed by Mesorah Publications, Inc., 4401 Second Avenue,
Brooklyn, NY 11232. Distributed in Israel by Sifriati/A. Gitler
Books, 6 Hayarkon Street, Bnai Brak 51127. Distributed in Europe
by Lehmanns, Unit E, Viking Industrial Park, Rolling Mill Road,
Jarow, NE32 3DP, England. Distributed in Australia and New Zealand
by Golds World of Judaica, 3-13 William Street, Balaclava, Melbourne
3183, Victoria, Australia. Distributed in South Africa by Kollel Bookshop,
8A Norwood Hypermarket, Norwood 2196, Johannesburg, South Africa.

ISBN 1-879016-15-X

PRINTED IN THE UNITED STATES OF AMERICA

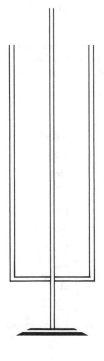

Guide to Reading the Transliteration

Consonants are to be read as they sound in English, except for the combination **ch** (ח, כ, ך) which is pronounced as in *challah*.

The "silent" Hebrew letters (א and ע) are not represented.

Vowels are to be pronounced as follows:

a	(ַ)	*as in*	hurr**ah**
o	(ָ)	*as in*	**o**ften
ō	(ֹ)	*as in*	p**o**st
ay	(ֵ)	*as in*	p**ay**
e	(ֶ)	*as in*	l**e**g
i	(ִ)	*as in*	mach**i**ne
u	(ֻ or וּ)	*as in*	l**u**nar
oy	(וֹי)	*as in*	b**oy**
ai	(ַי)	*as in*	**ai**sle

The sounded *sh'va* (ְ) is represented by ' and is pronounced similarly to the indistinct **a** in *ago*.

CONTENTS תוכן

SHABBOS AND FESTIVALS   סדר שבת ויום טוב

Candle Lighting for Shabbos	1	הַדְלָקַת הַנֵּרוֹת לְשַׁבָּת
Candle Lighting for Festivals	2	הַדְלָקַת הַנֵּרוֹת לְחַגִּים
Candle Lighting for Yom Kippur	3	הַדְלָקַת הַנֵּרוֹת לְיוֹם הַכִּפּוּרִים
Shalom Alaychem	4	שָׁלוֹם עֲלֵיכֶם
Ayshes Cha-yil	9	אֵשֶׁת־חַיִל
Blessing the Children	11	בִּרְכַּת הַבָּנִים
Kiddush for Friday Evening	12	קִדּוּשׁ לְלֵיל שַׁבָּת
Kiddush for Festival Evenings	14	קִדּוּשׁ לְלֵיל יוֹם טוֹב
Kiddush for Rosh Hashanah Evening	18	קִדּוּשׁ לְלֵיל רֹאשׁ הַשָּׁנָה
Kiddush for Shabbos Morning	22	קִדּוּשָׁא רַבָּה לְשַׁבָּת
Kiddush for Festival and Rosh Hashanah Mornings	24	קִדּוּשָׁא רַבָּה לְשָׁלֹשׁ רְגָלִים וּלְרֹאשׁ הַשָּׁנָה
Z'miros for Friday Evening	26	זְמִירוֹת לְלֵיל שַׁבָּת
Z'miros for Shabbos Morning	37	זְמִירוֹת לְיוֹם הַשַּׁבָּת
Z'miros for the Third Meal	49	זְמִירוֹת לִסְעוּדָה שְׁלִישִׁית
Havdoloh	53	הַבְדָּלָה

BLESSINGS   סדר ברכות

The Blessing After the Meal	59	בִּרְכַּת הַמָּזוֹן
The Blessing After a Snack	77	בְּרָכָה מֵעֵין שָׁלֹשׁ ("עַל הַמִּחְיָה")
The Blessing After a Wedding Meal	81	בִּרְכַּת הַמָּזוֹן לִסְעוּדַת נִשּׂוּאִין
The Blessing After the Meal Following a Circumcision	85	בִּרְכַּת הַמָּזוֹן לִבְרִית מִילָה
Blessings for All Occasions	91	בִּרְכוֹת הַנֶּהֱנִין, בִּרְכוֹת הַמִּצְווֹת, בִּרְכוֹת רְאִיָּה וּשְׁמִיעָה

POPULAR SONGS   97   שירי עם

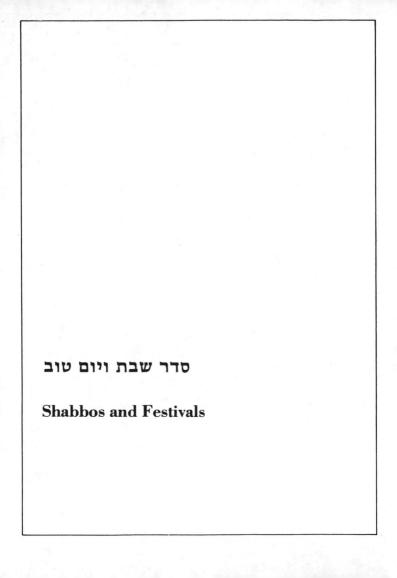

סדר שבת ויום טוב

Shabbos and Festivals

הַדְלָקַת הַנֵּרוֹת לְשַׁבָּת
CANDLE LIGHTING FOR SHABBOS

After lighting the Shabbos candles:

Boruch atoh adōnoy,　　　　　בָּרוּךְ אַתָּה יְיָ,

elōhaynu melech ho-ōlom,　　אֱלֹהֵינוּ מֶלֶךְ הָעוֹלָם,

asher kidshonu b'mitzvōsov　אֲשֶׁר קִדְּשָׁנוּ בְּמִצְוֹתָיו

v'tzivonu l'hadlik nayr　　　וְצִוָּנוּ לְהַדְלִיק נֵר

shel shabbos.　　　　　　　שֶׁל שַׁבָּת.

You are blessed, Lord our God, the sovereign of the world, who made us holy with His commandments and commanded us to kindle lights for Shabbos.

Y'hi rotzōn milfonecho, adōnoy　　יְהִי רָצוֹן מִלְּפָנֶיךָ, יְיָ

elōhaynu vaylōhay avōsaynu,　　אֱלֹהֵינוּ וֵאלֹהֵי אֲבוֹתֵינוּ,

sheyiboneh bays hamikdosh　　שֶׁיִּבָּנֶה בֵּית הַמִּקְדָּשׁ

bimhayroh v'yomaynu, v'sayn　בִּמְהֵרָה בְיָמֵינוּ, וְתֵן

chelkaynu b'sōrosecho. V'shom　חֶלְקֵנוּ בְּתוֹרָתֶךָ. וְשָׁם

na-avodcho b'yir-oh kimay　　נַעֲבָדְךָ בְּיִרְאָה כִּימֵי

ōlom uchshonim kadmōniyōs.　עוֹלָם וּכְשָׁנִים קַדְמוֹנִיּוֹת.

V'orvoh ladōnoy minchas y'hudoh　וְעָרְבָה לַיְיָ מִנְחַת יְהוּדָה

virusholoyim, kimay ōlom　　וִירוּשָׁלָיִם, כִּימֵי עוֹלָם

uchshonim kadmōniyōs.　　וּכְשָׁנִים קַדְמוֹנִיּוֹת.

May it be Your will, Lord our God and God of our fathers, that the Temple will be rebuilt soon in our time, and grant our involvement with Your Torah. And there we will serve You reverently as in days gone by, in olden times.

Y'hi rotzōn milfonecho, adōnoy　　יְהִי רָצוֹן מִלְּפָנֶיךָ, יְיָ

elōhai vaylōhay avōsai,　　אֱלֹהַי וֵאלֹהֵי אֲבוֹתַי,

shet-chōnayn ōsi (v'es　　שֶׁתְּחוֹנֵן אוֹתִי (וְאֶת-

ishi v'es bonai) v'es kol	אִישִׁי וְאֶת־בָּנַי) וְאֶת־כָּל־
k'rōvai v'sashlim botaynu	קְרוֹבַי וְתַשְׁלִים בָּתֵּינוּ
v'sashkayn sh'chinos-cho baynaynu.	וְתַשְׁכֵּן שְׁכִינָתְךָ בֵּינֵינוּ.
V'zakayni l'gadayl bonim uvnay	וְזַכֵּנִי לְגַדֵּל בָּנִים וּבְנֵי
vonim chachomim um-irim	בָנִים חֲכָמִים וּמְאִירִים
es ho-ōlom batōrah	אֶת־הָעוֹלָם בַּתּוֹרָה
uvma-asim tōvim v'ho-ayr	וּבְמַעֲשִׂים טוֹבִים וְהָאֵר
nayraynu shelō yichbeh l'ōlom	נֵרֵנוּ שֶׁלֹא יִכְבֶּה לְעוֹלָם
vo-ed. V'ho-ayr ponecho v'nivoshay-oh.	וָעֶד. וְהָאֵר פָּנֶיךָ וְנִוָּשֵׁעָה.
Omayn.	אָמֵן.

May it be Your will, Lord my God and God of my fathers, to be gracious to me (and to my husband and children) and to all my family, crowning our home with the feeling of Your divine presence dwelling among us. Make me worthy to raise learned children and grandchildren who will dazzle the world with Torah and goodness, and ensure that the glow of our lives will never be dimmed. Show us the glow of Your face and we will be saved. Amen.

הַדְלָקַת הַגֵּרוֹת לְחַגִּים
CANDLE LIGHTING FOR FESTIVALS

After lighting the candles:

Boruch atoh adōnoy,	בָּרוּךְ אַתָּה יְיָ,
elōhaynu melech ho-ōlom,	אֱלֹהֵינוּ מֶלֶךְ הָעוֹלָם,
asher kidshonu b'mitzvōsov	אֲשֶׁר קִדְּשָׁנוּ בְּמִצְוֹתָיו
v'tzivonu l'hadlik nayr shel	וְצִוָּנוּ לְהַדְלִיק נֵר שֶׁל
(shabbos v'shel)	(שַׁבָּת וְשֶׁל)
yōm tōv.	יוֹם טוֹב.

You are blessed, Lord our God, the sovereign of the world, who made us holy with His commandments and commanded us to kindle lights for (Shabbos and for) the festival.

Boruch atoh adōnoy,	בָּרוּךְ אַתָּה יְיָ,
elōhaynu melech ho-ōlom,	אֱלֹהֵינוּ מֶלֶךְ הָעוֹלָם,
shehecheyonu v'kiymonu v'higi-onu	שֶׁהֶחֱיָנוּ וְקִיְּמָנוּ וְהִגִּיעָנוּ
lazman hazeh.	לַזְּמַן הַזֶּה.
Y'hi rotzōn . . .	יְהִי רָצוֹן . . .

You are blessed, Lord our God, the sovereign of the world, who has kept us alive and sustained us and enabled us to reach this occasion.

May it be Your will . . .

הַדְלָקַת הַנֵּרוֹת לְיוֹם הַכִּפּוּרִים
CANDLE LIGHTING FOR YOM KIPPUR

After lighting the candles:

Boruch atoh adōnoy,	בָּרוּךְ אַתָּה יְיָ,
elōhaynu melech ho-ōlom,	אֱלֹהֵינוּ מֶלֶךְ הָעוֹלָם,
asher kidshonu b'mitzvōsov	אֲשֶׁר קִדְּשָׁנוּ בְּמִצְוֹתָיו
v'tzivonu l'hadlik nayr shel	וְצִוָּנוּ לְהַדְלִיק נֵר שֶׁל
(shabbos v'shel)	(שַׁבָּת וְשֶׁל)
yōm hakipurim.	יוֹם הַכִּפּוּרִים.

Boruch atoh adōnoy,	בָּרוּךְ אַתָּה יְיָ,
elōhaynu melech ho-ōlom,	אֱלֹהֵינוּ מֶלֶךְ הָעוֹלָם,
shehecheyonu v'kiymonu v'higi-onu	שֶׁהֶחֱיָנוּ וְקִיְּמָנוּ וְהִגִּיעָנוּ
lazman hazeh.	לַזְּמַן הַזֶּה.
Y'hi rotzōn . . .	יְהִי רָצוֹן . . .

You are blessed, Lord our God, the sovereign of the world, who made us holy with His commandments and commanded us to kindle lights for (Shabbos and for) Yom Kippur.

You are blessed, Lord our God, the sovereign of the world, who has kept us alive and sustained us and enabled us to reach this occasion.

May it be Your will . . .

שָׁלוֹם עֲלֵיכֶם
SHALOM ALAYCHEM

Sholōm alaychem mal-achay
hashorays mal-achay elyōn,
mimelech malchay hamlochim
hakodōsh boruch hu.

שָׁלוֹם עֲלֵיכֶם מַלְאֲכֵי
הַשָּׁרֵת מַלְאֲכֵי עֶלְיוֹן,
מִמֶּלֶךְ מַלְכֵי הַמְּלָכִים
הַקָּדוֹשׁ בָּרוּךְ הוּא.

Bō-achem l'sholōm mal-achay
hasholōm mal-achay elyōn,
mimelech malchay hamlochim
hakodōsh boruch hu.

בּוֹאֲכֶם לְשָׁלוֹם מַלְאֲכֵי
הַשָּׁלוֹם מַלְאֲכֵי עֶלְיוֹן,
מִמֶּלֶךְ מַלְכֵי הַמְּלָכִים
הַקָּדוֹשׁ בָּרוּךְ הוּא.

Borchuni l'sholōm mal-achay
hasholōm mal-achay elyōn,
mimelech malchay hamlochim
hakodōsh boruch hu.

בָּרְכוּנִי לְשָׁלוֹם מַלְאֲכֵי
הַשָּׁלוֹם מַלְאֲכֵי עֶלְיוֹן,
מִמֶּלֶךְ מַלְכֵי הַמְּלָכִים
הַקָּדוֹשׁ בָּרוּךְ הוּא.

Tzays'chem l'sholōm mal-achay
hasholōm mal-achay elyōn,
mimelech malchay hamlochim
hakodōsh boruch hu.

צֵאתְכֶם לְשָׁלוֹם מַלְאֲכֵי
הַשָּׁלוֹם מַלְאֲכֵי עֶלְיוֹן,
מִמֶּלֶךְ מַלְכֵי הַמְּלָכִים
הַקָּדוֹשׁ בָּרוּךְ הוּא.

Welcome, ministering angels, messengers of the Most High, of the supreme King of Kings, the Holy One, blessed be He.

Come in peace, messengers of peace, messengers of the Most High, of the supreme King of Kings, the Holy One, blessed be He.

Bless me with peace, messengers of peace, messengers of the Most High, of the supreme King of Kings, the Holy One, blessed be He.

And may your departure be in peace, messengers of peace, messengers of the Most High, of the supreme King of Kings, the Holy One, blessed be He.

Ki mal-ochov y'tzaveh loch,	כִּי מַלְאָכָיו יְצַוֶּה־לָךְ,
lishmorcho b'chol d'rochecho. Adonoy	לִשְׁמָרְךָ בְּכָל־דְּרָכֶיךָ. יְיָ
yishmor tzays'cho uvō-echo,	יִשְׁמָר־צֵאתְךָ וּבוֹאֶךָ,
may-atoh v'ad ōlom.	מֵעַתָּה וְעַד־עוֹלָם.

He will command His angels to watch over you in all your ways. The Lord will watch over your comings and goings from now on and forever more.

רִבּוֹן כָּל־הָעוֹלָמִים
RIBŌN KOL HO-ŌLOMIM

Ribōn kol ho-ōlomim, adōn kol	רִבּוֹן כָּל־הָעוֹלָמִים, אֲדוֹן כָּל־
hanshomōs, adon hasholōm, melech	הַנְּשָׁמוֹת, אֲדוֹן הַשָּׁלוֹם. מֶלֶךְ
abir, melech boruch, melech godōl,	אַבִּיר, מֶלֶךְ בָּרוּךְ, מֶלֶךְ גָּדוֹל,
melech dōvayr sholōm, melech hodur,	מֶלֶךְ דּוֹבֵר שָׁלוֹם, מֶלֶךְ הָדוּר,
melech vosik, melech zoch, melech chay	מֶלֶךְ וָתִיק, מֶלֶךְ זָךְ, מֶלֶךְ חַי
ho-olōmim, melech tōv umaytiv,	הָעוֹלָמִים, מֶלֶךְ טוֹב וּמֵטִיב,
melech yochid umyuchod, melech kabir,	מֶלֶךְ יָחִיד וּמְיֻחָד, מֶלֶךְ כַּבִּיר,
melech lōvaysh rachamim, melech	מֶלֶךְ לוֹבֵשׁ רַחֲמִים, מֶלֶךְ
malchay hamlochim melech nisgov,	מַלְכֵי הַמְּלָכִים, מֶלֶךְ נִשְׂגָּב,
melech sōmaych nōflim, melech	מֶלֶךְ סוֹמֵךְ נוֹפְלִים, מֶלֶךְ
ōsayh ma-asayh v'rayshis, melech	עוֹשֶׂה מַעֲשֵׂה בְרֵאשִׁית, מֶלֶךְ
pōdeh umatzil, melech tzach v'odōm,	פּוֹדֶה וּמַצִּיל, מֶלֶךְ צַח וְאָדוֹם,
melech kodōsh, melech rom v'niso,	מֶלֶךְ קָדוֹשׁ, מֶלֶךְ רָם וְנִשָּׂא,
melech shōmaya t'filoh,	מֶלֶךְ שׁוֹמֵעַ תְּפִלָּה,
melech tomim darkō.	מֶלֶךְ תָּמִים דַּרְכּוֹ.

Master of all worlds! Lord of all souls! Lord of peace! Mighty King, blessed King, great King, King who is synonymous with peace, glorious King, ancient King, pure King, King who is the life force of the universe, good and beneficent King, unique and singular King, powerful King, King robed in mercy, supreme King of Kings, sublime King, King who sustains the fallen,

King who is the author of creation, King who liberates and rescues, dazzling and ruddied King, holy King, exalted and elevated King, King who hears prayer, King whose way is flawless.

Modeh ani l'fonecho, adonoy elohai	מוֹדֶה אֲנִי לְפָנֶיךָ יְיָ אֱלֹהַי
vaylohay avosai, al kol hachesed	וֵאלֹהֵי אֲבוֹתַי עַל כָּל־הַחֶסֶד
asher osiso imodi, va-asher	אֲשֶׁר עָשִׂיתָ עִמָּדִי, וַאֲשֶׁר
atoh osid la-asos imi v'im	אַתָּה עָתִיד לַעֲשׂוֹת עִמִּי, וְעִם
kol b'nay vaysi v'im kol	כָּל־בְּנֵי בֵיתִי, וְעִם כָּל־
b'riyosecho, b'nai v'risi. Uvruchim	בְּרִיּוֹתֶיךָ, בְּנֵי בְרִיתִי. וּבְרוּכִים
haym malochecho hak'doshim	הֵם מַלְאָכֶיךָ הַקְּדוֹשִׁים
v'hat'horim she-osim r'tzonecho.	וְהַטְּהוֹרִים שֶׁעוֹשִׂים רְצוֹנֶךָ.
Adon hasholom, melech shehasholom	אֲדוֹן הַשָּׁלוֹם, מֶלֶךְ שֶׁהַשָּׁלוֹם
shelo, borchayni vasholom, v'sifkod	שֶׁלּוֹ, בָּרְכֵנִי בַשָּׁלוֹם, וְתִפְקֹד
osi v'es kol b'nay vaysi, v'chol	אוֹתִי וְאֶת־כָּל־בְּנֵי בֵיתִי, וְכָל־
amcho bays yisro-ayl l'chayim	עַמְּךָ בֵּית יִשְׂרָאֵל, לְחַיִּים
tovim ul'sholom.	טוֹבִים וּלְשָׁלוֹם.

I thank You, Lord my God and God of my fathers, for all the kindness with which You have treated me, and with which You will in the future treat me, my entire household, and all Your creatures who are associated with me. May Your holy and pure angels, who do Your bidding, be blessed. Lord of peace, King to whom peace belongs, bless me with peace, and consider me, my entire household, and all Your people the house of Israel, worthy of a life of well-being and peace.

Melech elyon al kol tz'vo	מֶלֶךְ עֶלְיוֹן עַל כָּל־צָבָא
morom, yotzraynu, yotzayr b'rayshis,	מָרוֹם. יוֹצְרֵנוּ, יוֹצֵר בְּרֵאשִׁית,
achaleh fonecho ham'irim,	אֲחַלֶּה פָנֶיךָ הַמְּאִירִים,
shet'zakeh osi v'es kol b'nay	שֶׁתְּזַכֶּה אוֹתִי וְאֶת־כָּל־בְּנֵי
vaysi limtzo chayn v'saychel tov	בֵיתִי לִמְצוֹא חֵן וְשֵׂכֶל טוֹב
b'aynecho uv'aynay chol b'nay odom,	בְּעֵינֶיךָ וּבְעֵינֵי כָל־בְּנֵי אָדָם,
uv'aynay chol ro-aynu, la-avodosecho.	וּבְעֵינֵי כָל־רוֹאֵינוּ, לַעֲבוֹדָתֶךָ.

6

V'zakaynu l'kabayl shabosōs mitōch	וְזַכֵּנוּ לְקַבֵּל שַׁבָּתוֹת מִתּוֹךְ
rōv simchoh, umitōch ōsher	רוֹב שִׂמְחָה, וּמִתּוֹךְ עשֶׁר
v'chovōd, umitōch mi-ut avōnōs;	וְכָבוֹד, וּמִתּוֹךְ מִיעוּט עֲוֹנוֹת.
v'hosayr mimeni umikol b'nay vaysi,	וְהָסֵר מִמֶּנִּי וּמִכָּל־בְּנֵי בֵיתִי,
umikol amcho bays yisro-ayl, kol	וּמִכָּל־עַמְּךָ בֵּית יִשְׂרָאֵל, כָּל־
minay chōli v'chol minay madveh,	מִינֵי חֳלִי וְכָל־מִינֵי מַדְוֶה,
v'chol minay dalus va-aniyus	וְכָל־מִינֵי דַלּוּת וַעֲנִיּוּת
v'evyōnus; v'sayn bonu yaytzer tōv	וְאֶבְיוֹנוּת. וְתֶן בָּנוּ יֵצֶר טוֹב
l'ovd'cho be-emes uv'yiroh	לְעָבְדְּךָ בֶּאֱמֶת וּבְיִרְאָה
uv'ahavoh. V'nih'yeh m'chubodim	וּבְאַהֲבָה. וְנִהְיֶה מְכֻבָּדִים
b'aynecho uv'aynay chol rō-aynu, ki	בְּעֵינֶיךָ וּבְעֵינֵי־כָל־רוֹאֵינוּ כִּי
atoh hu melech hakovōd, ki	אַתָּה הוּא מֶלֶךְ הַכָּבוֹד, כִּי
l'cho no-eh, ki l'cho yo-eh.	לְךָ נָאֶה, כִּי לְךָ יָאֶה.

King who is above the entire heavenly host, our creator, who formed the beginning of all things, I beseech Your resplendent countenance, to grant that I and my entire household find favor and understanding in Your sight, as well as in the sight of all men—all who see us—so that we may serve You. Make us worthy of welcoming Shabbos with great delight, enjoying wealth and respect, and free from too many sins. Keep all kinds of illness, pain, poverty, deprivation and destitution away from me and my entire household. Instill in us a positive desire to serve You with honesty, awe and love. May we commmand respect in Your sight and in the sight of all who see us, for You are the King of glory, for whom respect is seemly and appropriate.

Ono, melech malchay hamlochim,	אָנָּא, מֶלֶךְ מַלְכֵי הַמְּלָכִים,
tzavayh l'malochecho, malachay	צַוֵּה לְמַלְאָכֶיךָ, מַלְאֲכֵי
hashorays, m'shorsay elyōn,	הַשָּׁרֵת, מְשָׁרְתֵי עֶלְיוֹן,
sheyifk'duni b'rachamim, vivorchuni	שֶׁיִּפְקְדוּנִי בְּרַחֲמִים, וִיבָרְכוּנִי
b'vō-om l'vaysi b'yōm kodshaynu.	בְּבוֹאָם לְבֵיתִי בְּיוֹם קָדְשֵׁנוּ.
Ki hidlakti nayrōsai, v'hitzati	כִּי הִדְלַקְתִּי נֵרוֹתַי, וְהִצַּעְתִּי
mitosi, v'hechelafti simlōsai	מִטָּתִי, וְהֶחֱלַפְתִּי שִׂמְלוֹתַי
lichvōd yōm hashabos, uvosi	לִכְבוֹד יוֹם הַשַּׁבָּת, וּבָאתִי

l'vayscho l'hapil tchinosi l'fonecho	לְבֵיתְךָ לְהַפִּיל תְּחִנָּתִי לְפָנֶיךָ
sheta-avir anchosi, vo-o-id asher	שֶׁתַּעֲבִיר אַנְחָתִי, וָאָעִיד אֲשֶׁר
boroso b'shishoh yomim kol	בָּרָאתָ בְּשִׁשָּׁה יָמִים כָּל־
ha-y'tzur; v'eshneh va-ashalaysh ŏd	הַיְצוּר, וְאֶשְׁנֶה וַאֲשַׁלֵשׁ עוֹד
l'ho-id al kŏsi b'sŏch	לְהָעִיד עַל כּוֹסִי בְּתוֹךְ
simchosi, ka-asher tzivisani l'zochrŏ	שִׂמְחָתִי, כַּאֲשֶׁר צִוִּיתַנִי לְזָכְרוֹ
ulhisaneg b'yeser nishmosi asher	וּלְהִתְעַנֵג בְּיֶתֶר נִשְׁמָתִי אֲשֶׁר
nosato bi. Bŏ eshbŏs ka-asher	נָתַתָּ בִּי. בּוֹ אֶשְׁבּוֹת כַּאֲשֶׁר
tzivisani l'shorsecho, v'chayn agid	צִוִּיתַנִי לְשָׁרְתֶךָ, וְכֵן אַגִּיד
g'duloscho b'rinoh. V'shivisi adŏnoy	גְּדֻלָּתְךָ בְּרִנָּה. וְשִׁוִּיתִי יְיָ
likrosi, shet'rachamayni ŏd	לְקִרְאָתִי, שֶׁתְּרַחֲמֵנִי עוֹד
b'golusi lgo-olayni ul'orayr libi	בְּגָלוּתִי לְגָאֳלֵנִי וּלְעוֹרֵר לִבִּי
l'ahavosecho, v'oz eshmŏr pikudecho	לְאַהֲבָתֶךָ, וְאָז אֶשְׁמוֹר פִּקּוּדֶיךָ
v'chukecho b'li etzev, v'espalel	וְחֻקֶּיךָ בְּלִי עֶצֶב, וְאֶתְפַּלֵל
kados, koro-u-i uch'nochŏn.	כַּדָּת, כָּרָאוּי וּכְנָכוֹן.

Please, supreme King of Kings, instruct Your messengers, the ministering angels, the messengers of the Most High, to consider me mercifully, blessing me when they visit my house on our holy day. For I kindled my lights, prepared my bed and changed my clothes in honor of Shabbos. I went to Your house to entreat You to banish my tears. I testified that You formed all of creation in six days. Then I repeated it and I will again testify to it a third time over my cup—joyfully—in accordance with Your instruction to be mindful of Shabbos, enjoying the additional soul You have given me. I will rest on it, in accordance with Your instruction to serve You, and I will sing Your praises. I have established the Lord as my priority, in order that You should continue to be merciful towards me in my exile by redeeming me and arousing my heart's love for You so that I am able to observe Your bidding and Your laws free from distress, and to say my prayers in accordance with the halachah, appropriately and correctly.

Malachay hasholŏm, bŏ-achem	מַלְאֲכֵי הַשָּׁלוֹם, בּוֹאֲכֶם
l'sholŏm, borchuni l'sholŏm,	לְשָׁלוֹם, בָּרְכוּנִי לְשָׁלוֹם,

v'imru boruch l'shulchoni he-oruch,	וְאִמְרוּ בָּרוּךְ לְשֻׁלְחָנִי הֶעָרוּךְ,
v'tzayschem l'sholŏm, may-atoh v'ad	וְצֵאתְכֶם לְשָׁלוֹם, מֵעַתָּה וְעַד
ŏlom, omayn seloh.	עוֹלָם, אָמֵן סֶלָה.

Messengers of peace, come in peace, bless me with peace, pronounce a blessing over my Shabbos table, and depart peacefully, now and always. Amen. Selah.

אֵשֶׁת־חַיִל
AYSHES CHA-YIL

Ayshes cha-yil mi yimtzo	אֵשֶׁת־חַיִל מִי יִמְצָא
v'rochŏk mipninim michroh.	וְרָחֹק מִפְּנִינִים מִכְרָהּ.
Botach boh layv ba-loh	בָּטַח בָּהּ לֵב בַּעְלָהּ
v'sholol lŏ yechsor.	וְשָׁלָל לֹא יֶחְסָר.
G'molas-hu tŏv v'lŏ ro kŏl	גְּמָלַתְהוּ טוֹב וְלֹא־רָע כֹּל
y'may cha-yeho. Dorshoh tzemer	יְמֵי חַיֶּיהָ. דָּרְשָׁה צֶמֶר
ufishtim vata-as b'chayfetz	וּפִשְׁתִּים וַתַּעַשׂ בְּחֵפֶץ
kapeho. Hoysoh ko-oniyŏs	כַּפֶּיהָ. הָיְתָה כָּאֳנִיּוֹת
sŏchayr mimerchok tovi	סוֹחֵר מִמֶּרְחָק תָּבִיא
lachmoh. Vatokom b'ŏd	לַחְמָהּ. וַתָּקָם בְּעוֹד
lailoh vatitayn teref l'vaysoh	לַיְלָה וַתִּתֵּן טֶרֶף לְבֵיתָהּ
v'chŏk l'na-arŏseho. Zom'moh	וְחֹק לְנַעֲרֹתֶיהָ. זָמְמָה
sodeh vatikochayhu mipri	שָׂדֶה וַתִּקָּחֵהוּ מִפְּרִי
chapeho not-oh korem. Chogroh	כַפֶּיהָ נָטְעָה כָּרֶם. חָגְרָה
v'ŏz mosneho vat-amaytz	בְעוֹז מָתְנֶיהָ וַתְּאַמֵּץ
z'rŏ-ŏseho. To-amoh ki tŏv	זְרוֹעֹתֶיהָ. טָעֲמָה כִּי־טוֹב
sachroh lŏ yichbeh balailoh	סַחְרָהּ לֹא־יִכְבֶּה בַלַּיְלָה
nayroh. Yodeho shilchoh	נֵרָהּ. יָדֶיהָ שִׁלְּחָה
vakishŏr v'chapeho tomchu	בַכִּישׁוֹר וְכַפֶּיהָ תָּמְכוּ

folech. Kapoh porsoh le-oni	פָּלֶךְ. כַּפָּהּ פָּרְשָׂה לֶעָנִי
v'yodeho shilchoh lo-evyōn.	וְיָדֶיהָ שִׁלְּחָה לָאֶבְיוֹן.
Lō siro l'vaysoh misholeg	לֹא־תִירָא לְבֵיתָהּ מִשָּׁלֶג
ki chol baysoh lovush shonim.	כִּי כָל־בֵּיתָהּ לָבֻשׁ שָׁנִים.
Marvadim os'soh loh shaysh	מַרְבַדִּים עָשְׂתָה־לָּהּ שֵׁשׁ
v'argomon l'vushoh. Nōdo	וְאַרְגָּמָן לְבוּשָׁהּ. נוֹדָע
bash-orim ba-loh b'shivtō	בַּשְּׁעָרִים בַּעְלָהּ בְּשִׁבְתּוֹ
im ziknay oretz. Sodin	עִם־זִקְנֵי־אָרֶץ. סָדִין
os'soh vatimkōr vachagōr	עָשְׂתָה וַתִּמְכֹּר וַחֲגוֹר
nosnoh lakna-ani. Ōz v'hodor	נָתְנָה לַכְּנַעֲנִי. עֹז־וְהָדָר
l'vushoh vatis-chak l'yōm	לְבוּשָׁהּ וַתִּשְׂחַק לְיוֹם
acharōn. Piho pos-choh	אַחֲרוֹן. פִּיהָ פָּתְחָה
v'chochmoh v'sōras chesed al	בְחָכְמָה וְתוֹרַת־חֶסֶד עַל
l'shōnoh. Tzōfiyoh halichōs	לְשׁוֹנָהּ. צוֹפִיָּה הֲלִיכוֹת
baysoh v'lechem atzlus lō	בֵּיתָהּ וְלֶחֶם עַצְלוּת לֹא
sōchayl. Komu voneho	תֹאכֵל. קָמוּ בָנֶיהָ
vai-ashruho ba-loh vai-hal'loh.	וַיְאַשְּׁרוּהָ בַּעְלָהּ וַיְהַלְלָהּ.
Rabōs bonōs osu choyil	רַבּוֹת בָּנוֹת עָשׂוּ חָיִל
v'at olis al kulonoh.	וְאַתְּ עָלִית עַל־כֻּלָּנָה.
Sheker hachayn v'hevel hayōfi	שֶׁקֶר הַחֵן וְהֶבֶל הַיֹּפִי
ishoh yir-as adōnoy hi	אִשָּׁה יִרְאַת־יְיָ הִיא
sishalol. T'nu loh mipri	תִתְהַלָּל. תְּנוּ־לָהּ מִפְּרִי
yodeho vihal'luho vash-orim	יָדֶיהָ וִיהַלְלוּהָ בַשְּׁעָרִים
ma-aseho.	מַעֲשֶׂיהָ.

A good wife who can find? She is more precious than corals. Her husband places his trust in her and only profits thereby. She brings him good, not harm, all the days of her life. She seeks out wool and flax and cheerfully does the work of her hands. She is like the trading ships, bringing food from afar. She gets up while it is still night to provide food for her household, and a fair share for her staff. She considers a field and purchases it and plants a vineyard with the fruit of her labors. She invests herself with strength and makes her arms powerful. She senses that her trade is profitable; her light does not go out at night. She stretches out her hands to the distaff and her palms hold the spindle. She opens her hand to the poor and reaches out her hands to the needy. She has no fear of the snow for her household, for all her household is dressed in fine clothing. She makes her own coverlets; her clothing is of fine linen and luxurious cloth. Her husband is known at the gates, where he sits with the elders of the land. She makes and sells linens; she supplies the merchants with sashes. She is robed in strength and dignity and she smiles at the future. She opens her mouth with wisdom and the teaching of kindness is on her tongue. She looks after the conduct of her household and never tastes the bread of sloth. Her children rise up and make her happy; her husband praises her: "Many women have excelled, but you outshine them all!" Grace is elusive and beauty is vain, but a woman who fears the Lord—she shall be praised. Give her credit for the fruit of her labors and let her achievements praise her at the gates.

בִּרְכַּת הַבָּנִים
BLESSING THE CHILDREN

For a son:

Y'simcho elōhim
k'efrayim v'chimnasheh.

יְשִׂמְךָ אֱלֹהִים
כְּאֶפְרַיִם וְכִמְנַשֶּׁה.

May God make you like Ephraim and Menasseh.

For a daughter:

Y'simaych elōhim k'soroh,
rivkoh, rochayl v'lay-oh.

יְשִׂמֵךְ אֱלֹהִים כְּשָׂרָה,
רִבְקָה, רָחֵל וְלֵאָה.

May God make you like Sarah, Rebecca, Rachel and Leah.

For both continue:

Y'vorech'cho adōnoy v'yishm'recho.
Yo-ayr adōnoy ponov aylecho vichuneko.
Yiso adōnoy ponov aylecho,
v'yosaym l'cho sholōm.

יְבָרֶכְךָ יְיָ וְיִשְׁמְרֶךָ.
יָאֵר יְיָ פָּנָיו אֵלֶיךָ וִיחֻנֶּךָּ.
יִשָּׂא יְיָ פָּנָיו אֵלֶיךָ,
וְיָשֵׂם לְךָ שָׁלוֹם.

May the Lord bless you and watch over you. May the Lord shine His face towards you and show you favor. May the Lord be favorably disposed towards you and may He grant you peace.

קִדּוּשׁ לְלֵיל שַׁבָּת
KIDDUSH FOR FRIDAY EVENING

Kiddush is recited over a full cup of wine.

Vai-hi erev vai-hi vōker
yōm hashishi.

וַיְהִי־עֶרֶב וַיְהִי־בֹקֶר
יוֹם הַשִּׁשִּׁי.

Vai-chulu hashoma-yim v'ho-oretz
v'chol tz'vo-om. Vai-chal
elōhim bayōm hashvi-i
m'lach'tō asher osoh,
va-yishbōs ba-yōm hashvi-i
mikol m'lach'tō asher
osoh. Vai-vorech elōhim
es yōm hashvi-i vai-kadaysh
ōsō, ki vō shovas mikol
m'lach'tō asher boro
elōhim la-asōs.

וַיְכֻלּוּ הַשָּׁמַיִם וְהָאָרֶץ
וְכָל־צְבָאָם. וַיְכַל
אֱלֹהִים בַּיּוֹם הַשְּׁבִיעִי
מְלַאכְתּוֹ אֲשֶׁר עָשָׂה,
וַיִּשְׁבֹּת בַּיּוֹם הַשְּׁבִיעִי
מִכָּל־מְלַאכְתּוֹ אֲשֶׁר
עָשָׂה. וַיְבָרֶךְ אֱלֹהִים
אֶת־יוֹם הַשְּׁבִיעִי וַיְקַדֵּשׁ
אוֹתוֹ, כִּי בוֹ שָׁבַת מִכָּל־
מְלַאכְתּוֹ אֲשֶׁר בָּרָא
אֱלֹהִים לַעֲשׂוֹת.

It was evening and it was morning, the sixth day. So the heavens and the earth were finished, with all their complement. Thus, on the seventh day, God had completed His work which He had undertaken, and He rested on the seventh day from all His work which He had been doing. Then God blessed the seventh day and made it holy, because on it He rested from all His creative work, which God had brought into being to fulfill its purpose.

Sovray moronon v'rabonon v'rabōsai:

סָבְרֵי מָרָנָן וְרַבָּנָן וְרַבּוֹתַי:

Boruch atoh adōnoy,
elōhaynu melech ho-ōlom,
bōray p'ri hagofen.

בָּרוּךְ אַתָּה יְיָ,
אֱלֹהֵינוּ מֶלֶךְ הָעוֹלָם,
בּוֹרֵא פְּרִי הַגָּפֶן.

You are blessed, Lord our God, the sovereign of the world, creator of the fruit of the vine.

	בָּרוּךְ אַתָּה יְיָ,
Boruch atoh adōnoy,	אֱלֹהֵינוּ מֶלֶךְ הָעוֹלָם,
elōhaynu melech ho-ōlom,	אֲשֶׁר קִדְּשָׁנוּ בְּמִצְוֹתָיו
asher kidshonu b'mitzvōsov	וְרָצָה בָנוּ, וְשַׁבַּת קָדְשׁוֹ
v'rotzoh vonu, v'shabbas kodshō	בְּאַהֲבָה וּבְרָצוֹן הִנְחִילָנוּ,
b'ahavoh uvrotzōn hinchilonu,	זִכָּרוֹן לְמַעֲשֵׂה בְרֵאשִׁית.
zikorōn l'ma-asayh v'rayshis.	כִּי הוּא יוֹם תְּחִלָּה
Ki hu yōm t'chiloh	לְמִקְרָאֵי קֹדֶשׁ, זֵכֶר
l'mikro-ay kōdesh, zaycher	לִיצִיאַת מִצְרָיִם. כִּי־בָנוּ
litzi-as mitzroyim. Ki vonu	בָחַרְתָּ וְאוֹתָנוּ קִדַּשְׁתָּ
vocharto v'ōsonu kidashto	מִכָּל־הָעַמִּים, וְשַׁבַּת
mikol ho-amim, v'shabbas	קָדְשְׁךָ בְּאַהֲבָה וּבְרָצוֹן
kodsh'cho b'ahavoh uvrotzōn	הִנְחַלְתָּנוּ. בָּרוּךְ אַתָּה יְיָ,
hinchaltonu. Boruch atoh adōnoy,	מְקַדֵּשׁ הַשַּׁבָּת.
m'kadaysh hashabbos.	

You are blessed, Lord our God, the sovereign of the world, who made us holy with His commandments and favored us, and gave us His holy Shabbos, in love and favor, to be our heritage, as a reminder of the Creation. It is the foremost day of the holy festivals marking the exodus from Egypt. For—out of all the nations—You chose us and made us holy, and You gave us Your holy Shabbos, in love and favor, as our heritage. You are blessed, Lord, who sanctifies Shabbos.

קִדּוּשׁ לְלֵיל יוֹם טוֹב
KIDDUSH FOR FESTIVAL EVENINGS

Kiddush is recited over a full cup of wine.

On Shabbos begin here:

Vai-hi erev vai-hi vōker
yōm hashishi.

וַיְהִי־עֶרֶב וַיְהִי־בֹקֶר
יוֹם הַשִּׁשִׁי.

Vai-chulu hashoma-yim v'ho-oretz
v'chol tz'vo-om. Vai-chal
elōhim bayōm hashvi-i
m'lach'tō asher osoh,
va-yishbōs ba-yōm hashvi-i
mikol m'lach'tō asher
osoh. Vai-vorech elōhim
es yōm hashvi-i vai-kadaysh
ōsō, ki vō shovas mikol
m'lach'tō asher boro
elōhim la-asōs.

וַיְכֻלּוּ הַשָּׁמַיִם וְהָאָרֶץ
וְכָל־צְבָאָם. וַיְכַל
אֱלֹהִים בַּיּוֹם הַשְּׁבִיעִי
מְלַאכְתּוֹ אֲשֶׁר עָשָׂה,
וַיִּשְׁבֹּת בַּיּוֹם הַשְּׁבִיעִי
מִכָּל־מְלַאכְתּוֹ אֲשֶׁר
עָשָׂה. וַיְבָרֶךְ אֱלֹהִים
אֶת־יוֹם הַשְּׁבִיעִי וַיְקַדֵּשׁ
אוֹתוֹ, כִּי בוֹ שָׁבַת מִכָּל־
מְלַאכְתּוֹ אֲשֶׁר בָּרָא
אֱלֹהִים לַעֲשׂוֹת.

It was evening and it was morning, the sixth day. So the heavens and the earth were finished, with all their complement. Thus, on the seventh day, God had completed His work which He had undertaken, and He rested on the seventh day from all His work which He had been doing. Then God blessed the seventh day and made it holy, because on it He rested from all His creative work, which God had brought into being to fulfill its purpose.

On other evenings begin here:

Sovray moronon v'rabonon v'rabōsai:

סָבְרִי מָרָנָן וְרַבָּנָן וְרַבּוֹתַי:

Boruch atoh adōnoy,
elōhaynu melech ho-ōlom,
bōray p'ri hagofen.

בָּרוּךְ אַתָּה יְיָ,
אֱלֹהֵינוּ מֶלֶךְ הָעוֹלָם,
בּוֹרֵא פְּרִי הַגָּפֶן.

You are blessed, Lord our God, the sovereign of the world, creator of the fruit of the vine.

Boruch atoh adōnoy,	בָּרוּךְ אַתָּה יְיָ,
elōhaynu melech ho-ōlom,	אֱלֹהֵינוּ מֶלֶךְ הָעוֹלָם,
asher bochar bonu mikol om,	אֲשֶׁר בָּחַר בָּנוּ מִכָּל־עָם,
v'rōm'monu mikol loshōn,	וְרוֹמְמָנוּ מִכָּל־לָשׁוֹן,
v'kidshonu b'mitzvōsov.	וְקִדְּשָׁנוּ בְּמִצְוֹתָיו.
Vatiten lonu, adōnoy	וַתִּתֶּן־לָנוּ, יְיָ
elōhaynu, b'ahavoh	אֱלֹהֵינוּ, בְּאַהֲבָה
(shabbosōs limnuchoh u)	(שַׁבָּתוֹת לִמְנוּחָה וּ)
mō-adim l'simchoh, chagim	מוֹעֲדִים לְשִׂמְחָה, חַגִּים
uzmanim l'sosōn, es yōm	וּזְמַנִּים לְשָׂשׂוֹן, אֶת־יוֹם
(hashabbos hazeh, v'es yōm)	(הַשַּׁבָּת הַזֶּה, וְאֶת־יוֹם)

on Pesach

chag hamatzōs hazeh,	חַג הַמַּצּוֹת הַזֶּה,
z'man chayrusaynu,	זְמַן חֵרוּתֵנוּ,

on Shavuos

chag hashovu-ōs hazeh,	חַג הַשָּׁבֻעוֹת הַזֶּה,
z'man matan tōrosaynu,	זְמַן מַתַּן תּוֹרָתֵינוּ,

on Sukkos

chag hasukōs hazeh,	חַג הַסֻּכּוֹת הַזֶּה,
z'man simchosaynu	זְמַן שִׂמְחָתֵנוּ

on Sh'mini Atzeres and Simchas Torah

hashmini, chag ho-atzeres	הַשְּׁמִינִי, חַג הָעֲצֶרֶת
hazeh, z'man simchosaynu,	הַזֶּה, זְמַן שִׂמְחָתֵנוּ,
(b'ahavoh) mikro kōdesh,	(בְּאַהֲבָה) מִקְרָא קֹדֶשׁ,
zaycher litzi-as mitzroyim. Ki	זֵכֶר לִיצִיאַת מִצְרָיִם. כִּי־
vonu vocharto v'ōsonu kidashto	בָנוּ בָחַרְתָּ וְאוֹתָנוּ קִדַּשְׁתָּ

mikol ho-amim, (v'shabbos)	מִכָּל־הָעַמִּים, (וְשַׁבָּת)
umō-aday kodsh'cho (b'ahavoh	וּמוֹעֲדֵי קָדְשֶׁךָ (בְּאַהֲבָה
uvrotzōn) b'simchoh uvsosōn	וּבְרָצוֹן) בְּשִׂמְחָה וּבְשָׂשׂוֹן
hinchaltonu. Boruch atoh adōnoy,	הִנְחַלְתָּנוּ. בָּרוּךְ אַתָּה יְיָ,
m'kadaysh (hashabbos v')	מְקַדֵּשׁ (הַשַּׁבָּת וְ)
yisro-ayl v'hazmanim.	יִשְׂרָאֵל וְהַזְּמַנִּים.

You are blessed, Lord our God, the sovereign of the world, who chose us out of all the nations, and exalted us above all peoples, and made us holy with His commandments. You gave us, Lord our God, with love (Shabbos for rest and) set times for joy, festivals and holidays for happiness: this (Shabbos and this) Festival day of

Pesach/Shavuos/Sukkos/Sh'mini Atzeres

(with love), a sacred assembly marking the exodus from Egypt. For—out of all the nations—You chose us and made us holy, and You gave us Your holy (Shabbos and) festivals (in love and favor) for joy and for happiness, as our heritage. You are blessed, Lord, who sanctifies (Shabbos,) Israel and the holidays.

On Saturday night add:

Boruch atoh adōnoy,	בָּרוּךְ אַתָּה יְיָ,
elōhaynu melech ho-ōlom,	אֱלֹהֵינוּ מֶלֶךְ הָעוֹלָם,
bōray m'ōray ho-aysh.	בּוֹרֵא מְאוֹרֵי הָאֵשׁ.

You are blessed, Lord our God, the sovereign of the world, creator of the lights of fire.

Boruch atoh adōnoy,	בָּרוּךְ אַתָּה יְיָ,
elōhaynu melech ho-ōlom,	אֱלֹהֵינוּ מֶלֶךְ הָעוֹלָם,
hamavdil bayn kōdesh l'chōl,	הַמַּבְדִּיל בֵּין קֹדֶשׁ לְחֹל,
bayn ōr l'chōshech, bayn	בֵּין אוֹר לְחֹשֶׁךְ, בֵּין
yisro-ayl lo-amim, bayn yōm	יִשְׂרָאֵל לָעַמִּים, בֵּין יוֹם
hashvi-i l'shayshes y'may	הַשְּׁבִיעִי לְשֵׁשֶׁת יְמֵי
hama-aseh. Bayn k'dushas	הַמַּעֲשֶׂה. בֵּין קְדֻשַׁת
shabbos likdushas yōm tōv	שַׁבָּת לִקְדֻשַּׁת יוֹם טוֹב

hivdalto, v'es yōm	הִבְדַּלְתָּ, וְאֶת־יוֹם
hashvi-i mishayshes y'may	הַשְּׁבִיעִי מִשֵּׁשֶׁת יְמֵי
hama-aseh kidashto. Hivdalto	הַמַּעֲשֶׂה קִדַּשְׁתָּ. הִבְדַּלְתָּ
v'kidashto es amcho yisro-ayl	וְקִדַּשְׁתָּ אֶת־עַמְּךָ יִשְׂרָאֵל
bikdushosecho. Boruch atoh adōnoy,	בִּקְדֻשָּׁתֶךָ. בָּרוּךְ אַתָּה יְיָ,
hamavdil bayn kōdesh l'kōdesh.	הַמַּבְדִּיל בֵּין קֹדֶשׁ לְקֹדֶשׁ.

You are blessed, Lord our God, the sovereign of the world, who makes a distinction between sacred and secular, between light and darkness, between Israel and the other nations, between the seventh day and the six working days. You made a distinction between the holiness of Shabbos and the holiness of a festival, just as You made the seventh day holier than the six working days. You have set levels of holiness for Your people Israel through Your sanctity. You are blessed, Lord, who sets different levels of holiness.

Omit on the last two evenings of Pesach:

Boruch atoh adōnoy,	בָּרוּךְ אַתָּה יְיָ,
elōhaynu melech ho-ōlom,	אֱלֹהֵינוּ מֶלֶךְ הָעוֹלָם,
shehecheyonu v'kiymonu v'higi-onu	שֶׁהֶחֱיָנוּ וְקִיְּמָנוּ וְהִגִּיעָנוּ
lazman hazeh.	לַזְּמַן הַזֶּה.

You are blessed, Lord our God, the sovereign of the world, who has kept us alive and sustained us and enabled us to reach this occasion.

In the sukkah add:

Boruch atoh adōnoy,	בָּרוּךְ אַתָּה יְיָ,
elōhaynu melech ho-ōlom,	אֱלֹהֵינוּ מֶלֶךְ הָעוֹלָם,
asher kidshonu b'mitzvōsov	אֲשֶׁר קִדְּשָׁנוּ בְּמִצְוֹתָיו
v'tzivonu layshayv basukoh.	וְצִוָּנוּ לֵשֵׁב בַּסֻּכָּה.

You are blessed, Lord our God, the sovereign of the world, who made us holy with His commandments and commanded us to live in the succah.

(On the first evening of Sukkos only, say this blessing
***before* the preceding one.)**

קִדּוּשׁ לְלֵיל רֹאשׁ הַשָּׁנָה
KIDDUSH FOR ROSH HASHANAH EVENING

Kiddush is recited over a full cup of wine.

On Shabbos begin here:

Vai-hi erev vai-hi vōker	וַיְהִי־עֶרֶב וַיְהִי־בֹקֶר
yōm hashishi.	יוֹם הַשִּׁשִּׁי.
Vai-chulu hashoma-yim v'ho-oretz	וַיְכֻלּוּ הַשָּׁמַיִם וְהָאָרֶץ
v'chol tz'vo-om. Vai-chal	וְכָל־צְבָאָם. וַיְכַל
elōhim bayōm hashvi-i	אֱלֹהִים בַּיּוֹם הַשְּׁבִיעִי
m'lach'tō asher osoh,	מְלַאכְתּוֹ אֲשֶׁר עָשָׂה,
va-yishbōs bayōm hashvi-i	וַיִּשְׁבֹּת בַּיּוֹם הַשְּׁבִיעִי
mikol m'lach'tō asher	מִכָּל־מְלַאכְתּוֹ אֲשֶׁר
osoh. Vai-vorech elōhim	עָשָׂה. וַיְבָרֶךְ אֱלֹהִים
es yōm hashvi-i vai-kadaysh	אֶת־יוֹם הַשְּׁבִיעִי וַיְקַדֵּשׁ
ōsō, ki vō shovas mikol	אוֹתוֹ, כִּי בוֹ שָׁבַת מִכָּל־
m'lach'tō asher boro	מְלַאכְתּוֹ אֲשֶׁר בָּרָא
elōhim la-asōs.	אֱלֹהִים לַעֲשׂוֹת.

It was evening and it was morning, the sixth day. So the heavens and the earth were finished, with all their complement. Thus, on the seventh day, God had completed His work which He had undertaken, and He rested on the seventh day from all His work which He had been doing. Then God blessed the seventh day and made it holy, because on it He rested from all His creative work, which God had brought into being to fulfill its purpose.

On other evenings begin here:

Sovray moronon v'rabonon v'rabōsai:	סַבְרִי מָרָנָן וְרַבָּנָן וְרַבּוֹתַי:
Boruch atoh adōnoy,	בָּרוּךְ אַתָּה יְיָ,
elōhaynu melech ho-ōlom,	אֱלֹהֵינוּ מֶלֶךְ הָעוֹלָם,
bōray p'ri hagofen.	בּוֹרֵא פְּרִי הַגָּפֶן.

18

You are blessed, Lord our God, the sovereign of the world, creator of the fruit of the vine.

Boruch atoh adōnoy,	בָּרוּךְ אַתָּה יְיָ,
elōhaynu melech ho-ōlom,	אֱלֹהֵינוּ מֶלֶךְ הָעוֹלָם,
asher bochar bonu mikol om,	אֲשֶׁר בָּחַר בָּנוּ מִכָּל־עָם,
v'rōm'monu mikol loshōn,	וְרוֹמְמָנוּ מִכָּל־לָשׁוֹן,
v'kidshonu b'mitzvōsov.	וְקִדְּשָׁנוּ בְּמִצְוֹתָיו.
Vatiten lonu, adōnoy	וַתִּתֶּן־לָנוּ, יְיָ
elōhaynu, b'ahavoh es yōm	אֱלֹהֵינוּ, בְּאַהֲבָה אֶת־יוֹם
(hashabbos hazeh v'es yōm)	(הַשַּׁבָּת הַזֶּה וְאֶת־יוֹם)
hazikorōn hazeh, yōm (zichrōn)	הַזִּכָּרוֹן הַזֶּה, יוֹם (זִכְרוֹן)
t'ru-oh (b'ahavoh) mikro	תְּרוּעָה (בְּאַהֲבָה) מִקְרָא
kōdesh, zaycher litzi-as	קֹדֶשׁ, זֵכֶר לִיצִיאַת
mitzroyim. Ki vonu vocharto	מִצְרָיִם. כִּי־בָנוּ בָחַרְתָּ
v'ōsonu kidashto mikol	וְאוֹתָנוּ קִדַּשְׁתָּ מִכָּל־
ho-amim, udvorcho emes	הָעַמִּים, וּדְבָרְךָ אֱמֶת
v'kayom lo-ad. Boruch atoh adōnoy,	וְקַיָּם לָעַד. בָּרוּךְ אַתָּה יְיָ,
melech al kol ho-oretz,	מֶלֶךְ עַל כָּל־הָאָרֶץ,
m'kadaysh (hashabbos v')	מְקַדֵּשׁ (הַשַּׁבָּת וְ)
yisro-ayl v'yōm hazikorōn.	יִשְׂרָאֵל וְיוֹם הַזִּכָּרוֹן.

You are blessed, Lord our God, the sovereign of the world, who chose us out of all the nations, and exalted us above all peoples, and made us holy with His commandments. You gave us, Lord our God, with love this (Shabbos day and this) Day of Remembrance, a day for (mentioning) blowing the shofar, a sacred assembly marking the exodus from Egypt. For—out of all the nations—You chose us and made us holy, and your word is true and reliable forever. You are blessed, Lord, the king of the whole earth who sanctifies (Shabbos,) Israel and the Day of Remembrance.

Boruch atoh adōnoy,	בָּרוּךְ אַתָּה יְיָ,
elōhaynu melech ho-ōlom,	אֱלֹהֵינוּ מֶלֶךְ הָעוֹלָם,
bōray m'ōray ho-aysh.	בּוֹרֵא מְאוֹרֵי הָאֵשׁ.

You are blessed, Lord our God, the sovereign of the world, creator of the lights of fire.

Boruch atoh adōnoy,	בָּרוּךְ אַתָּה יְיָ,
elōhaynu melech ho-ōlom,	אֱלֹהֵינוּ מֶלֶךְ הָעוֹלָם,
hamavdil bayn kōdesh l'chōl,	הַמַּבְדִּיל בֵּין קֹדֶשׁ לְחֹל,
bayn ōr l'chōshech,	בֵּין אוֹר לְחֹשֶׁךְ,
bayn yisro-ayl lo-amim,	בֵּין יִשְׂרָאֵל לָעַמִּים,
bayn yōm hashvi-i	בֵּין יוֹם הַשְּׁבִיעִי
l'shayshes y'may hama-aseh. Bayn	לְשֵׁשֶׁת יְמֵי הַמַּעֲשֶׂה. בֵּין
k'dushas shabbos likdushas yōm	קְדֻשַּׁת שַׁבָּת לִקְדֻשַּׁת יוֹם
tōv hivdalto, v'es yōm	טוֹב הִבְדַּלְתָּ, וְאֶת־יוֹם
hashvi-i mishayshes y'may	הַשְּׁבִיעִי מִשֵּׁשֶׁת יְמֵי
hama-aseh kidashto. Hivdalto	הַמַּעֲשֶׂה קִדַּשְׁתָּ. הִבְדַּלְתָּ
v'kidashto es amcho yisro-ayl	וְקִדַּשְׁתָּ אֶת־עַמְּךָ יִשְׂרָאֵל
bikdushosecho. Boruch atoh adōnoy,	בִּקְדֻשָּׁתֶךָ. בָּרוּךְ אַתָּה יְיָ,
hamavdil bayn kōdesh l'kōdesh.	הַמַּבְדִּיל בֵּין קֹדֶשׁ לְקֹדֶשׁ.

You are blessed, Lord our God, the sovereign of the world, who makes a distinction between sacred and secular, between light and darkness, between Israel and the other nations, between the seventh day and the six working days. You made a distinction between the holiness of Shabbos and the holiness of a festival, just as You made the seventh day holier than the six working days. You have set levels of holiness for Your people Israel through Your sanctity. You are blessed, Lord, who sets different levels of holiness.

On both evenings continue here:

Boruch atoh adōnoy,	בָּרוּךְ אַתָּה יְיָ,
elōhaynu melech ho-ōlom,	אֱלֹהֵינוּ מֶלֶךְ הָעוֹלָם,

shehecheyonu v'kiymonu v'higi-onu
lazman hazeh.

שֶׁהֶחֱיָנוּ וְקִיְּמָנוּ וְהִגִּיעָנוּ
לַזְּמַן הַזֶּה.

You are blessed, Lord our God, the sovereign of the world, who has kept us alive and sustained us and enabled us to reach this occasion.

Following Kiddush there is a custom to eat a piece of apple dipped in honey, expressing the wish that the New Year should be a sweet one.

Boruch atoh adōnoy,

elōhaynu melech ho-ōlom,

bōray p'ri ho-aytz.

בָּרוּךְ אַתָּה יְיָ,
אֱלֹהֵינוּ מֶלֶךְ הָעוֹלָם,
בּוֹרֵא פְּרִי הָעֵץ.

You are blessed, Lord our God, the sovereign of the world, creator of the fruit of trees.

After eating some of the apple, say the following:

Y'hi rotzōn milfonecho adōnoy

elōhaynu vaylōhay avōsaynu

shet-chadaysh olaynu shonoh

tōvoh umsukoh.

יְהִי רָצוֹן מִלְפָנֶיךָ יְיָ
אֱלֹהֵינוּ וֵאלֹהֵי אֲבוֹתֵינוּ
שֶׁתְּחַדֵּשׁ עָלֵינוּ שָׁנָה
טוֹבָה וּמְתוּקָה.

May it be Your will, Lord our God and God of our fathers, that You give us a good and sweet New Year.

קִדּוּשָׁא רַבָּה לְשַׁבָּת
KIDDUSH FOR SHABBOS MORNING

V'shomru v'nay yisro-ayl	וְשָׁמְרוּ בְנֵי־יִשְׂרָאֵל
es hashabbos, la-asōs	אֶת־הַשַּׁבָּת, לַעֲשׂוֹת
es hashabbos l'dōrōsom b'ris	אֶת־הַשַּׁבָּת לְדֹרֹתָם בְּרִית
ōlom. Bayni uvayn	עוֹלָם. בֵּינִי וּבֵין
b'nay yisro-ayl ōs hi	בְּנֵי־יִשְׂרָאֵל אוֹת הִיא
l'ōlom, ki shayshes yomim	לְעוֹלָם, כִּי שֵׁשֶׁת יָמִים
osoh adōnoy es hashoma-yim	עָשָׂה יְיָ אֶת־הַשָּׁמַיִם
v'es ho-oretz uva-yōm	וְאֶת־הָאָרֶץ וּבַיּוֹם
hashvi-i shovas va-yinofash.	הַשְּׁבִיעִי שָׁבַת וַיִּנָּפַשׁ.
Zochōr es yōm hashabbos	זָכוֹר אֶת־יוֹם הַשַּׁבָּת
l'kadshō. Shayshes yomim	לְקַדְּשׁוֹ. שֵׁשֶׁת יָמִים
ta-avōd v'osiso kol	תַּעֲבֹד וְעָשִׂיתָ כָּל־
m'lach'techo. V'yōm hashvi-i	מְלַאכְתֶּךָ. וְיוֹם הַשְּׁבִיעִי
shabbos ladōnoy elōhecho, lō	שַׁבָּת לַיָי אֱלֹהֶיךָ, לֹא־
sa-aseh chol m'lochoh atoh	תַעֲשֶׂה כָל־מְלָאכָה אַתָּה
uvincho uvitecho avd'cho vo-amos-cho	וּבִנְךָ וּבִתֶּךָ עַבְדְּךָ וַאֲמָתְךָ
uvhemtecho v'gayrcho asher	וּבְהֶמְתֶּךָ וְגֵרְךָ אֲשֶׁר
bish-orecho. Ki shayshes yomim	בִּשְׁעָרֶיךָ. כִּי שֵׁשֶׁת־יָמִים
osoh adōnoy es hashoma-yim	עָשָׂה יְיָ אֶת־הַשָּׁמַיִם
v'es ho-oretz es ha-yom	וְאֶת־הָאָרֶץ אֶת־הַיָּם
v'es kol asher bom, va-yonach	וְאֶת־כָּל־אֲשֶׁר־בָּם וַיָּנַח
ba-yōm hashvi-i,	בַּיּוֹם הַשְּׁבִיעִי,
al kayn bayrach adōnoy es yōm	עַל־כֵּן בֵּרַךְ יְיָ אֶת־יוֹם
hashabbos vai-kadshayhu.	הַשַּׁבָּת וַיְקַדְּשֵׁהוּ.

22

The children of Israel should keep Shabbos, observing Shabbos throughout their generations, as an everlasting covenant. It is a sign between Me and the children of Israel for all time, that in six days the Lord made the heavens and the earth, and that on the seventh day He was finished and He rested.

Be mindful of Shabbos, to make it holy. You should labor for six days and do all your work, but the seventh day is Shabbos for the Lord your God. You may not do any creative work—neither you nor your son, nor your daughter, nor your male or female worker, nor your cattle, nor the stranger who dwells among you. Because it was in six days that the Lord made the heavens and the earth, the sea, and all that they contain, and He rested on the seventh day.

That is why the Lord blessed Shabbos and made it holy.

Sovray moronon v'rabonon v'rabōsai: סָבְרִי מָרָנָן וְרַבָּנָן וְרַבּוֹתַי:

For wine:

Boruch atoh adōnoy,   בָּרוּךְ אַתָּה יְיָ,
elōhaynu melech ho-ōlom,   אֱלֹהֵינוּ מֶלֶךְ הָעוֹלָם,
bōray p'ri hagofen.   בּוֹרֵא פְּרִי הַגָּפֶן.

You are blessed, Lord our God, the sovereign of the world, creator of the fruit of the vine.

For other drinks:

Boruch atoh adōnoy,   בָּרוּךְ אַתָּה יְיָ,
elōhaynu melech ho-ōlom,   אֱלֹהֵינוּ מֶלֶךְ הָעוֹלָם,
shehakōl nihyeh bidvorō.   שֶׁהַכֹּל נִהְיֶה בִּדְבָרוֹ.

You are blessed, Lord our God, the sovereign of the world, through whose word everything came into being.

קִדּוּשָׁא רַבָּה לְשָׁלֹשׁ רְגָלִים וּלְרֹאשׁ הַשָּׁנָה
KIDDUSH FOR FESTIVAL AND
ROSH HASHANAH MORNINGS

On Shabbos begin here:

V'shomru v'nay yisro-ayl	וְשָׁמְרוּ בְנֵי־יִשְׂרָאֵל
es hashabbos, la-asōs	אֶת־הַשַּׁבָּת, לַעֲשׂוֹת
es hashabbos l'dōrōsom b'ris	אֶת־הַשַּׁבָּת לְדֹרֹתָם בְּרִית
ōlom. Bayni uvayn	עוֹלָם. בֵּינִי וּבֵין
b'nay yisro-ayl ōs hi	בְּנֵי־יִשְׂרָאֵל אוֹת הִיא
l'ōlom, ki shayshes yomim	לְעוֹלָם, כִּי שֵׁשֶׁת יָמִים
osoh adōnoy es hashoma-yim	עָשָׂה יְיָ אֶת־הַשָּׁמַיִם
v'es ho-oretz uva-yōm	וְאֶת־הָאָרֶץ וּבַיּוֹם
hashvi-i shovas va-yinofash.	הַשְּׁבִיעִי שָׁבַת וַיִּנָּפַשׁ.

The children of Israel should keep Shabbos, observing Shabbos throughout their generations, as an everlasting covenant. It is a sign between Me and the children of Israel for all time, that in six days the Lord made the heavens and the earth, and that on the seventh day he was finished and He rested.

On a weekday begin here:

For Pesach, Shavuos, Sukkos, Sh'mini Atzeres and Simchas Torah

Ayleh mō-aday adōnoy, mikro-ay	אֵלֶּה מוֹעֲדֵי יְיָ, מִקְרָאֵי
kōdesh, asher tikr'u	קֹדֶשׁ, אֲשֶׁר תִּקְרְאוּ
ōsom b'mō-adom. Vai-dabayr	אוֹתָם בְּמוֹעֲדָם. וַיְדַבֵּר
mōsheh es mō-aday adōnoy el	מֹשֶׁה אֶת־מוֹעֲדֵי יְיָ אֶל
b'nay yisro-ayl.	בְּנֵי יִשְׂרָאֵל.

These are the set times of the Lord, sacred assemblies, which you shall proclaim in their appointed seasons. So Moses told the children of Israel about the set times of the Lord.

For Rosh Hashanah

Tiku vachōdesh shōfor,
bakeseh l'yōm chagaynu. Ki chōk
l'yisro-ayl hu, mishpot
laylōhay ya-akōv.

תִּקְעוּ בַחֹדֶשׁ שׁוֹפָר,
בַּכֶּסֶה לְיוֹם חַגֵּנוּ. כִּי חֹק
לְיִשְׂרָאֵל הוּא, מִשְׁפָּט
לֵאלֹהֵי יַעֲקֹב.

Blow the shofar in that month, at the full moon for our festive day. For it
is a statute of Israel, an ordinance of the God of Jacob.

Sovray moronon v'rabonon v'rabōsai:

סָבְרֵי מָרָנָן וְרַבָּנָן וְרַבּוֹתַי:

For wine:

Boruch atoh adōnoy,
elōhaynu melech ho-ōlom,
bōray p'ri hagofen.

בָּרוּךְ אַתָּה יְיָ,
אֱלֹהֵינוּ מֶלֶךְ הָעוֹלָם,
בּוֹרֵא פְּרִי הַגָּפֶן.

You are blessed, Lord our God, the sovereign of the world, creator of the
fruit of the vine.

For other drinks:

Boruch atoh adōnoy,
elōhaynu melech ho-ōlom,
shehakōl nihyeh bidvorō.

בָּרוּךְ אַתָּה יְיָ,
אֱלֹהֵינוּ מֶלֶךְ הָעוֹלָם,
שֶׁהַכֹּל נִהְיֶה בִּדְבָרוֹ.

You are blessed, Lord our God, the sovereign of the world, by whose word
everything came into being.

In the sukkah add:

Boruch atoh adōnoy,
elōhaynu melech ho-ōlom,
asher kidshonu b'mitzvōsov
v'tzivonu layshayv basukoh.

בָּרוּךְ אַתָּה יְיָ,
אֱלֹהֵינוּ מֶלֶךְ הָעוֹלָם,
אֲשֶׁר קִדְּשָׁנוּ בְּמִצְוֹתָיו
וְצִוָּנוּ לֵשֵׁב בַּסֻּכָּה.

You are blessed, Lord our God, the sovereign of the world, who made us
holy with His commandments and commanded us to live in the succah.

זְמִירוֹת לְלֵיל שַׁבָּת
ZEMIROS FOR FRIDAY EVENING

1 *Kol m'kadaysh sh'vi-i*   כָּל־מְקַדֵּשׁ שְׁבִיעִי

Whoever keeps Shabbos will receive his due reward. Shabbos is a gift from God; it is to be warmly welcomed and enjoyed. May those who observe the laws of Shabbos enjoy God's support.

Kol m'kadaysh sh'vi-i koro-ui	כָּל־מְקַדֵּשׁ שְׁבִיעִי כָּרָאוּי
lō, kol shōmayr shabbos kados	לוֹ, כָּל־שֹׁמֵר שַׁבָּת כַּדָּת
maychal'lō, s'chorō harbayh	מֵחַלְּלוֹ, שְׂכָרוֹ הַרְבֵּה
m'ōd al pi fo-olō, ish	מְאֹד עַל־פִּי פָעֳלוֹ, אִישׁ
al machanayhu v'ish	עַל־מַחֲנֵהוּ וְאִישׁ
al diglō.	עַל־דִּגְלוֹ.
Ōhavay adōnoy hamchakim l'vinyan	אוֹהֲבֵי יְיָ הַמְחַכִּים לְבִנְיַן
ari-ayl, b'yōm hashabbos	אֲרִיאֵל, בְּיוֹם הַשַּׁבָּת
sisu v'simchu kimkablay matan	שִׂישׂוּ וְשִׂמְחוּ כִּמְקַבְּלֵי מַתַּן
nachali-ayl, gam s'u y'daychem	נַחֲלִיאֵל, גַּם שְׂאוּ־יְדֵיכֶם
kōdesh v'imru lo-ayl, boruch	קֹדֶשׁ וְאִמְרוּ לָאֵל, בָּרוּךְ
adōnoy asher nosan m'nuchoh	יְיָ אֲשֶׁר נָתַן מְנוּחָה
l'amō yisro-ayl.	לְעַמּוֹ יִשְׂרָאֵל.
Dōrshay adōnoy zera avrohom	דּוֹרְשֵׁי יְיָ זֶרַע אַבְרָהָם
ōhavō, ham-acharim lotzays	אֹהֲבוֹ, הַמְאַחֲרִים לָצֵאת
min hashabbos um'maharim	מִן הַשַּׁבָּת וּמְמַהֲרִים
lovō, usmaychim l'shomrō	לָבֹא, וּשְׂמֵחִים לְשָׁמְרוֹ
ul-orayv ayruvō, zeh ha-yōm	וּלְעָרֵב עֵרוּבוֹ, זֶה־הַיּוֹם
osoh adōnoy nogiloh	עָשָׂה יְיָ נָגִילָה
v'nism'choh vō.	וְנִשְׂמְחָה בוֹ.

26

<table>
<tr><td>

Zichru tōras mōsheh b'mitzvas
shabbos g'rusoh, charusoh
la-yōm hashvi-i k'chaloh bayn
ray-ōseho m'shubotzoh,
t'hōrim yiroshuho
vikadshuho b'ma-amar kol
asher osoh, vai-chal elōhim
ba-yōm hashvi-i m'lach'tō
asher osoh.

</td><td dir="rtl">

זִכְרוּ תּוֹרַת מֹשֶׁה בְּמִצְוַת
שַׁבָּת גְּרוּסָה, חֲרוּתָה
לַיּוֹם הַשְּׁבִיעִי כְּכַלָּה בֵּין
רֵעוֹתֶיהָ מְשֻׁבָּצָה,
טְהוֹרִים יִירָשׁוּהָ
וִיקַדְּשׁוּהָ בְּמַאֲמַר כָּל־
אֲשֶׁר עָשָׂה, וַיְכַל אֱלֹהִים
בַּיּוֹם הַשְּׁבִיעִי מְלַאכְתּוֹ
אֲשֶׁר עָשָׂה.

</td></tr>
<tr><td>

Yōm kodōsh hu mibō-ō
v'ad tzaysō, kol zera ya-akōv
y'chabduhu kidvar hamelech
v'dosō, lonuach bō v'lismōach
b'sa-anug ochōl v'shosō, kol
adas yisro-ayl ya-asu ōsō.

</td><td dir="rtl">

יוֹם קָדוֹשׁ הוּא מִבֹּאוֹ
וְעַד צֵאתוֹ, כָּל־זֶרַע יַעֲקֹב
יְכַבְּדוּהוּ כִּדְבַר הַמֶּלֶךְ
וְדָתוֹ, לָנוּחַ בּוֹ וְלִשְׂמֹחַ
בְּתַעֲנוּג אָכוֹל וְשָׁתוֹ, כָּל־
עֲדַת יִשְׂרָאֵל יַעֲשׂוּ אוֹתוֹ.

</td></tr>
<tr><td>

M'shōch chasd'cho l'yōd-echo ayl
kanō v'nōkaym, nōtray yōm
hashvi-i zochōr v'shomōr
l'hokaym, samchaym b'vinyan
sholaym uv-ōr ponecho
tavhikaym, yirv'yun mideshen
baysecho v'nachal adonecho
sashkaym.

</td><td dir="rtl">

מְשֹׁךְ חַסְדְּךָ לְיֹדְעֶיךָ אֵל
קַנּוֹא וְנֹקֵם, נוֹטְרֵי יוֹם
הַשְּׁבִיעִי זָכוֹר וְשָׁמוֹר
לְהָקֵם, שַׂמְּחֵם בְּבִנְיַן
שָׁלֵם וּבְאוֹר פָּנֶיךָ
תַּבְהִיקֵם, יִרְוְיֻן מִדֶּשֶׁן
בֵּיתֶךָ וְנַחַל עֲדָנֶיךָ
תַשְׁקֵם.

</td></tr>
<tr><td>

Azōr lashōvsim bashvi-i
bechorish uvakotzir
l'ōlomim, pōs-im bō
p'si-oh k'tanoh sō-adim bō
l'voraych sholosh p'omim,

</td><td dir="rtl">

עֲזוֹר לַשּׁוֹבְתִים בַּשְּׁבִיעִי
בֶּחָרִישׁ וּבַקָּצִיר
לְעוֹלָמִים, פּוֹסְעִים בּוֹ
פְּסִיעָה קְטַנָּה סוֹעֲדִים בּוֹ
לְבָרֵךְ שָׁלֹשׁ פְּעָמִים,

</td></tr>
</table>

tzidkosom tatzhir k'ōr shiv-as ha-yomim, adōnoy elōhay yisro-ayl hovoh somim, adōnoy elōhay yisro-ayl t'shu-as ōlomim.	צִדְקָתָם תַּצְהִיר כְּאוֹר שִׁבְעַת הַיָּמִים, יְיָ אֱלֹהֵי יִשְׂרָאֵל הָבָה תָמִים, יְיָ אֱלֹהֵי יִשְׂרָאֵל תְּשׁוּעַת עוֹלָמִים.

2 M'nuchoh v'simchoh

מְנוּחָה וְשִׂמְחָה

By observing Shabbos we acknowledge that the world and all it contains were created by God in six days. Everything is special on Shabbos, from the prayers we recite to the food we eat. Enjoy it—you will be richly rewarded!

M'nuchoh v'simchoh ōr lai-hudim, yōm shabbosōn yōm machamadim, shōmrov v'zōchrov haymoh m'idim, ki l'shishoh kōl b'ru-im v'ōmdim.	מְנוּחָה וְשִׂמְחָה אוֹר לַיְהוּדִים, יוֹם שַׁבָּתוֹן יוֹם מַחֲמַדִּים, שׁוֹמְרָיו וְזֹכְרָיו הֵמָּה מְעִידִים, כִּי לְשִׁשָּׁה כֹל בְּרוּאִים וְעוֹמְדִים.
Sh'may shoma-yim eretz v'yamim, kol tz'vo morōm g'vōhim v'romim, tanin v'odom v'cha-yas r'aymim, ki b'yoh adōnoy tzur ōlomim.	שְׁמֵי שָׁמַיִם אֶרֶץ וְיַמִּים, כָּל-צְבָא מָרוֹם גְּבֹהִים וְרָמִים, תַּנִּין וְאָדָם וְחַיַּת רְאֵמִים, כִּי בְּיָהּ יְיָ צוּר עוֹלָמִים.
Hu asher diber l'am s'gulosō, shomōr l'kadshō mibō-ō v'ad tzaysō, shabbas kōdesh yōm chemdosō, ki vō shovas mikol m'lach'tō.	הוּא אֲשֶׁר דִּבֶּר לְעַם סְגֻלָּתוֹ, שָׁמוֹר לְקַדְּשׁוֹ מִבֹּאוֹ וְעַד-צֵאתוֹ, שַׁבַּת קֹדֶשׁ יוֹם חֶמְדָּתוֹ, כִּי בוֹ שָׁבַת מִכָּל-מְלַאכְתּוֹ.
B'mitzvas shabbos ayl yachalitzoch, kum k'ro aylov	בְּמִצְוַת שַׁבָּת אֵל יַחֲלִיצָךְ, קוּם קְרָא אֵלָיו

28

yochish l'amtzoch, nishmas	יָחִישׁ לְאַמְצָךְ, נִשְׁמַת
kol chai v'gam na-aritzoch, echōl	כָּל־חַי וְגַם נַעֲרִיצָךְ, אֱכֹל
b'simchoh ki k'vor rotzoch.	בְּשִׂמְחָה כִּי כְּבָר רָצָךְ.

B'mishneh lechem v'kidush	בְּמִשְׁנֶה לֶחֶם וְקִדּוּשׁ
raboh, b'rōv mat-amim v'ruach	רַבָּה, בְּרֹב מַטְעַמִּים וְרוּחַ
n'divoh, yizku l'rav tuv	נְדִיבָה, יִזְכּוּ לְרַב טוּב
hamis-angim boh, b'vi-as	הַמִּתְעַנְּגִים בָּהּ, בְּבִיאַת
gō-ayl l'cha-yay ho-ōlom habo.	גּוֹאֵל לְחַיֵּי הָעוֹלָם הַבָּא.

3 *Mah y'didus m'nuchosaych* מַה יְדִידוּת מְנוּחָתֵךְ

Shabbos Queen! How beloved you are to us. We run to greet you, to kindle the lights and to enjoy all sorts of wonderful delicacies at your three meals. We desist from our regular occupations. We should spend special time with our children and take care that the atmosphere should be relaxed and generally delightful. Truly, Shabbos is a taste of the world to come.

Mah y'didus m'nuchosaych, at	מַה־יְדִידוּת מְנוּחָתֵךְ, אַתְּ
shabbos hamalkoh, b'chayn norutz	שַׁבָּת הַמַּלְכָּה, בְּכֵן נָרוּץ
likrosaych, bō-i chaloh	לִקְרָאתֵךְ, בּוֹאִי כַלָּה
n'suchoh, l'vush bigday	נְסוּכָה, לְבוּשׁ בִּגְדֵי
chamudōs, l'hadlik nayr	חֲמוּדוֹת, לְהַדְלִיק נֵר
bivrochoh, vataychel kol	בִּבְרָכָה, וַתֵּכֶל כָּל־
ho-avōdōs, lō sa-asu	הָעֲבוֹדוֹת, לֹא תַעֲשׂוּ
m'lochoh.	מְלָאכָה.

L'his-anayg b'sa-anugim,	לְהִתְעַנֵּג בְּתַעֲנוּגִים,
barburim uslov v'dogim.	בַּרְבּוּרִים וּשְׂלָו וְדָגִים.

May-erev mazminim, kol minay	מֵעֶרֶב מַזְמִינִים, כָּל־מִינֵי
mat-amim, mib-ōd yōm	מַטְעַמִּים, מִבְּעוֹד יוֹם

muchonim, tarn'gōlim	מוּכָנִים, תַּרְנְגוֹלִים
m'futomim, v'la-arōch kamoh	מְפֻטָּמִים, וְלַעֲרוֹךְ כַּמָּה
minim, sh'sōs yaynōs	מִינִים, שְׁתוֹת יֵינוֹת
m'vushomim, v'safnukay	מְבֻשָּׂמִים, וְתַפְנוּקֵי
ma-adanim, b'chol sholosh	מַעֲדַנִּים, בְּכָל־שָׁלֹשׁ
p'omim.	פְּעָמִים.
L'his-anayg b'sa-anugim,	לְהִתְעַנֵּג בְּתַעֲנוּגִים,
barburim uslov v'dogim.	בַּרְבּוּרִים וּשְׂלָו וְדָגִים.
Nachalas ya-akōv yirosh, b'li	נַחֲלַת יַעֲקֹב יִירָשׁ, בְּלִי־
m'tzorim nachaloh, vichabduhu	מְצָרִים נַחֲלָה, וִיכַבְּדוּהוּ
oshir vorosh, v'sizku	עָשִׁיר וָרָשׁ, וְתִזְכּוּ
lig-uloh, yōm shabbos im	לִגְאֻלָּה, יוֹם שַׁבָּת אִם־
tishmōru, vihyisem li	תִּשְׁמֹרוּ, וִהְיִיתֶם לִי
s'guloh, shayshes yomim	סְגֻלָּה, שֵׁשֶׁת יָמִים
ta-avōdu, uvashvi-i nogiloh.	תַּעֲבֹדוּ, וּבַשְּׁבִיעִי נָגִילָה.
L'his-anayg b'sa-anugim,	לְהִתְעַנֵּג בְּתַעֲנוּגִים,
barburim uslov v'dogim.	בַּרְבּוּרִים וּשְׂלָו וְדָגִים.
Chafotzecho asurim, v'gam	חֲפָצֶיךָ אֲסוּרִים, וְגַם
lachashōv cheshbōnōs,	לַחֲשֹׁב חֶשְׁבּוֹנוֹת,
hirhurim mutorim,	הִרְהוּרִים מֻתָּרִים,
ulshadaych habonōs, v'sinōk	וּלְשַׁדֵּךְ הַבָּנוֹת, וְתִינוֹק
l'lamdō sayfer, lamnatzayach	לְלַמְּדוֹ סֵפֶר, לַמְנַצֵּחַ
binginōs, v'lahagōs	בִּנְגִינוֹת, וְלַהֲגוֹת
b'imray shefer,	בְּאִמְרֵי שֶׁפֶר,
b'chol pinōs umachanōs.	בְּכָל־פִּנּוֹת וּמַחֲנוֹת.
L'his-anayg b'sa-anugim,	לְהִתְעַנֵּג בְּתַעֲנוּגִים,
barburim uslov v'dogim.	בַּרְבּוּרִים וּשְׂלָו וְדָגִים.

Hiluchoch t'hay v'nachas, ōneg	הֲלוּכָךְ תְּהֵא בְנַחַת, עֹנֶג
k'ro lashabbos, v'hashaynoh	קְרָא לַשַּׁבָּת, וְהַשֵּׁנָה
m'shubachas, kados nefesh	מְשֻׁבַּחַת, כַּדָּת נֶפֶשׁ
m'shivas, b'chayn nafshi l'cho	מְשִׁיבַת, בְּכֵן נַפְשִׁי לְךָ
orgoh, v'lonuach b'chibas,	עָרְגָה, וְלָנוּחַ בְּחִבַּת,
kashōshanim sugoh,	כַּשּׁוֹשַׁנִּים סוּגָה,
bō yonuchu bayn uvas.	בּוֹ יָנוּחוּ בֵּן וּבַת.
L'his-anayg b'sa-anugim,	לְהִתְעַנֵּג בְּתַעֲנוּגִים,
barburim uslov v'dogim.	בַּרְבּוּרִים וּשְׂלָו וְדָגִים.
May-ayn ōlom habo, yōm	מֵעֵין עוֹלָם הַבָּא, יוֹם
shabbos m'nuchoh, kol	שַׁבָּת מְנוּחָה, כָּל־
hamis-angim boh, yizku l'rōv	הַמִּתְעַנְּגִים בָּהּ, יִזְכּוּ לְרֹב
simchoh, maychevlay moshiyach	שִׂמְחָה, מֵחֶבְלֵי מָשִׁיחַ
yutzolu lirvochoh, p'dusaynu	יָצְלוּ לִרְוָחָה, פְּדוּתֵנוּ
satzmiyach, v'nos yogōn va-anochoh.	תַצְמִיחַ, וְנָס יָגוֹן וַאֲנָחָה.
L'his-anayg b'sa-anugim,	לְהִתְעַנֵּג בְּתַעֲנוּגִים,
barburim uslov v'dogim.	בַּרְבּוּרִים וּשְׂלָו וְדָגִים.

4 *Yōm zeh l'yisro-ayl*	יוֹם זֶה לְיִשְׂרָאֵל

This is Israel's special day, a day of light, of happiness and of rest, as You commanded us on Mount Sinai. It refreshes us with the gift of an extra soul. You made the world in six days and told us not to work on the seventh day. We know we will be rewarded if we keep Shabbos, but, please God, do not forget that the Temple is still to be rebuilt.

Yōm zeh l'yisro-ayl ōroh	יוֹם זֶה לְיִשְׂרָאֵל אוֹרָה
v'simchoh, shabbas m'nuchoh.	וְשִׂמְחָה, שַׁבָּת מְנוּחָה.

Tziviso pikudim b'ma-amad	צִוִּיתָ פִּקוּדִים בְּמַעֲמַד
sinai, shabbos umō-adim	סִינַי, שַׁבָּת וּמוֹעֲדִים
lishmōr b'chol shonai, la-arōch	לִשְׁמוֹר בְּכָל־שָׁנַי, לַעֲרוֹךְ
l'fonai, mas-ays va-aruchoh,	לְפָנַי, מַשְׂאֵת וַאֲרוּחָה,
shabbos m'nuchoh.	שַׁבָּת מְנוּחָה.

Yōm zeh l'yisro-ayl ōroh	יוֹם זֶה לְיִשְׂרָאֵל אוֹרָה
v'simchoh, shabbas m'nuchoh.	וְשִׂמְחָה, שַׁבָּת מְנוּחָה.

Chemdas halvovōs l'umoh	חֶמְדַּת הַלְּבָבוֹת לְאֻמָּה
sh'vuroh, linfoshōs	שְׁבוּרָה, לִנְפָשׁוֹת
nich-ovōs n'shomoh y'sayroh,	נִכְאָבוֹת נְשָׁמָה יְתֵרָה,
l'nefesh m'tzayroh yosir anochoh,	לְנֶפֶשׁ מְצֵרָה יָסִיר אֲנָחָה,
shabbas m'nuchoh.	שַׁבָּת מְנוּחָה.

Yōm zeh l'yisro-ayl ōroh	יוֹם זֶה לְיִשְׂרָאֵל אוֹרָה
v'simchoh, shabbas m'nuchoh.	וְשִׂמְחָה, שַׁבָּת מְנוּחָה.

Kidashto bayrachto ōsō	קִדַּשְׁתָּ בֵּרַכְתָּ אוֹתוֹ
mikol yomim, b'shayshes kiliso	מִכָּל־יָמִים, בְּשֵׁשֶׁת כִּלִּיתָ
m'leches ōlomim, bō	מְלֶאכֶת עוֹלָמִים, בּוֹ
motzu agumim hashkayt	מָצְאוּ עֲגוּמִים הַשְׁקֵט
uvit-choh, shabbas m'nuchoh.	וּבִטְחָה, שַׁבָּת מְנוּחָה.

Yōm zeh l'yisro-ayl ōroh	יוֹם זֶה לְיִשְׂרָאֵל אוֹרָה
v'simchoh, shabbas m'nuchoh.	וְשִׂמְחָה, שַׁבָּת מְנוּחָה.

L'isur m'lochoh tzivisonu	לְאִסּוּר מְלָאכָה צִוִּיתָנוּ
nōro, ezkeh hōd m'luchoh	נוֹרָא, אֶזְכֶּה הוֹד מְלוּכָה
im shabbos eshmōroh,	אִם שַׁבָּת אֶשְׁמֹרָה,
akriv shai lamōro minchoh	אַקְרִיב שַׁי לַמּוֹרָא מִנְחָה
merkochoh, shabbas m'nuchoh.	מֶרְקָחָה, שַׁבָּת מְנוּחָה.

Yōm zeh l'yisro-ayl ōroh
v'simchoh, shabbas m'nuchoh.

יוֹם זֶה לְיִשְׂרָאֵל אוֹרָה
וְשִׂמְחָה, שַׁבַּת מְנוּחָה.

Chadaysh mikdoshaynu zochroh
nechereves, tuvcho mōshi-aynu
t'noh lane-etzeves, b'shabbos
yōsheves bizmir ushvochoh,
shabbas m'nuchoh.

חַדֵּשׁ מִקְדָּשֵׁנוּ זָכְרָה
נֶחֱרֶבֶת, טוּבְךָ מוֹשִׁיעֵנוּ
תְּנָה לַנֶּעֱצֶבֶת, בְּשַׁבָּת
יוֹשֶׁבֶת בְּזָמִיר וּשְׁבָחָה,
שַׁבַּת מְנוּחָה.

Yōm zeh l'yisro-ayl ōroh
v'simchoh, shabbas m'nuchoh.

יוֹם זֶה לְיִשְׂרָאֵל אוֹרָה
וְשִׂמְחָה, שַׁבַּת מְנוּחָה.

5 *Yoh ribōn*

יָה רִבּוֹן

Lord of all worlds! All Your creatures praise You. Even if we lived a
thousand years, we could not recount the extent of Your greatness. God,
save Your people from their exile and rebuild the Temple, and there, in
Jerusalem, we will really be able to sing to You!

Yoh ribōn olam v'olma-yo,
ant' hu malko melech
malcha-yo. Ōvad g'vurtaych
v'simha-yo, sh'far kodomoch
l'hachavoyoh.

יָה רִבּוֹן עָלַם וְעָלְמַיָּא,
אַנְתְּ הוּא מַלְכָּא מֶלֶךְ
מַלְכַיָּא. עוֹבַד גְּבוּרְתֵּךְ
וְתִמְהַיָּא, שְׁפַר קֳדָמָךְ
לְהַחֲוָיָה.

Sh'vochin asadayr tzafro
v'ramsho, loch eloho
kadisho di v'ro chol
nafsho, irin kadishin
uvnay enosho, chayvas boro
v'ōfay sh'ma-yo.

שְׁבָחִין אֲסַדֵּר צַפְרָא
וְרַמְשָׁא, לָךְ אֱלָהָא
קַדִּישָׁא דִּי בְרָא כָל-
נַפְשָׁא, עִירִין קַדִּישִׁין
וּבְנֵי אֱנָשָׁא, חֵיוַת בָּרָא
וְעוֹפֵי שְׁמַיָּא.

Yoh ribōn olam v'olma-yo,	יָהּ רִבּוֹן עָלַם וְעָלְמַיָּא,
ant' hu malko	אַנְתְּ הוּא מַלְכָּא
melech malcha-yo.	מֶלֶךְ מַלְכַיָּא.
Ravr'vin ōvdoch v'sakifin,	רַבְרְבִין עוֹבְדָיךְ וְתַקִּיפִין,
mochaych roma-yo v'zokayf k'fifin,	מָכֵךְ רָמַיָּא וְזָקֵף כְּפִיפִין,
lu yechyay g'var sh'nin	לוּ יְחֵא גְּבַר שְׁנִין
alfin, lo yay-ōl g'vurtaych	אַלְפִין, לָא יֵעֹל גְּבוּרְתֵּךְ
b'chushb'na-yo.	בְּחֻשְׁבְּנַיָּא.
Yoh ribōn olam v'olma-yo,	יָהּ רִבּוֹן עָלַם וְעָלְמַיָּא,
ant' hu malko	אַנְתְּ הוּא מַלְכָּא
melech malcha-yo.	מֶלֶךְ מַלְכַיָּא.
Eloho di layh y'kor	אֱלָהָא דִי לֵהּ יְקָר
urvuso, p'rōk yos onoch	וּרְבוּתָא, פְּרֹק יָת־עָנָךְ
mipum aryovoso, v'apayk yos	מִפֻּם אַרְיָוָתָא, וְאַפֵּק יָת
amoch migō goluso, amoch di	עַמָּךְ מִגּוֹ גָלוּתָא, עַמָּךְ דִי
v'chart' mikol uma-yo.	בְחַרְתְּ מִכָּל־אֻמַּיָּא.
Yoh ribōn olam v'olma-yo,	יָהּ רִבּוֹן עָלַם וְעָלְמַיָּא,
ant' hu malko	אַנְתְּ הוּא מַלְכָּא
melech malcha-yo.	מֶלֶךְ מַלְכַיָּא.
L'mikd'shoch tuv ulkōdesh	לְמִקְדְּשָׁךְ תּוּב וּלְקֹדֶשׁ
kudshin, asar di vayh	קֻדְשִׁין, אֲתַר דִּי בֵהּ
yechedun ruchin v'nafshin,	יֶחֱדוּן רוּחִין וְנַפְשִׁין,
vizamrun loch shirin	וִיזַמְּרוּן לָךְ שִׁירִין
v'rachashin, birushlaym karto	וְרַחֲשִׁין, בִּירוּשְׁלֵם קַרְתָּא
d'shufra-yo.	דְשֻׁפְרַיָּא.

34

Yoh ribōn olam v'olma-yo,	יָהּ רִבּוֹן עָלַם וְעָלְמַיָּא,
ant' hu malko	אַנְתְּ הוּא מַלְכָּא
melech malcha-yo.	מֶלֶךְ מַלְכַיָּא.

6   Tzur mishelō ochalnu   צוּר מִשֶּׁלּוֹ אָכַלְנוּ

My friends, let us bless God whose food we have eaten. He feeds the world and deserves our praise. God, have mercy on us and send the Messiah. Rebuild the Temple and we will sing a new song over a cup brimming with wine.

Tzur mishelō ochalnu, borchu	צוּר מִשֶּׁלּוֹ אָכַלְנוּ, בָּרְכוּ
emunai, sova-nu v'hōsarnu,	אֱמוּנַי, שָׂבַעְנוּ וְהוֹתַרְנוּ,
kidvar adōnoy.	כִּדְבַר יְיָ.
Hazon es ōlomō, rō-aynu	הַזָּן אֶת־עוֹלָמוֹ, רוֹעֵנוּ
ovinu, ochalnu es lachmō,	אָבִינוּ, אָכַלְנוּ אֶת־לַחְמוֹ,
v'yaynō shosinu, al kayn nōdeh	וְיֵינוֹ שָׁתִינוּ, עַל־כֵּן נוֹדֶה
lishmō, unhal'lō b'finu,	לִשְׁמוֹ, וּנְהַלְלוֹ בְּפִינוּ,
omarnu v'oninu,	אָמַרְנוּ וְעָנִינוּ,
ayn kodōsh kaadōnoy.	אֵין־קָדוֹשׁ כַּיְיָ.
Tzur mishelō ochalnu, borchu	צוּר מִשֶּׁלּוֹ אָכַלְנוּ, בָּרְכוּ
emunai, sova-nu v'hōsarnu,	אֱמוּנַי, שָׂבַעְנוּ וְהוֹתַרְנוּ,
kidvar adōnoy.	כִּדְבַר יְיָ.
B'shir v'kōl tōdoh, n'voraych	בְּשִׁיר וְקוֹל תּוֹדָה, נְבָרֵךְ
elōhaynu, al eretz chemdoh,	אֱלֹהֵינוּ, עַל אֶרֶץ חֶמְדָּה,
shehinchil la-avōsaynu, mozōn	שֶׁהִנְחִיל לַאֲבוֹתֵינוּ, מָזוֹן
v'tzaydoh, hisbi-a l'nafshaynu,	וְצֵידָה, הִשְׂבִּיעַ לְנַפְשֵׁנוּ,
chasdō govar olaynu,	חַסְדּוֹ גָּבַר עָלֵינוּ,
ve-emes adōnoy.	וֶאֱמֶת יְיָ.

Tzur mishelō ochalnu, borchu
emunai, sova-nu v'hōsarnu,
kidvar adōnoy.

צוּר מִשֶּׁלוֹ אָכַלְנוּ, בָּרְכוּ
אֱמוּנַי, שָׂבַעְנוּ וְהוֹתַרְנוּ,
כִּדְבַר יְיָ.

Rachaym b'chasdecho, al amcho
tzuraynu, al tziyōn mishkan
k'vōdecho, z'vul bays
tif-artaynu, ben dovid avdecho,
yovō v'yig-olaynu, ruach apaynu,
m'shiyach adōnoy.

רַחֵם בְּחַסְדֶּךָ, עַל עַמְּךָ
צוּרֵנוּ, עַל צִיּוֹן מִשְׁכַּן
כְּבוֹדֶךָ, זְבוּל בֵּית
תִּפְאַרְתֵּנוּ, בֶּן־דָּוִד עַבְדֶּךָ,
יָבֹא וְיִגְאָלֵנוּ, רוּחַ אַפֵּינוּ,
מְשִׁיחַ יְיָ.

Tzur mishelō ochalnu, borchu
emunai, sova-nu v'hōsarnu,
kidvar adōnoy.

צוּר מִשֶּׁלוֹ אָכַלְנוּ, בָּרְכוּ
אֱמוּנַי, שָׂבַעְנוּ וְהוֹתַרְנוּ,
כִּדְבַר יְיָ.

Yiboneh hamikdosh, ir tziyōn
t'malay, v'shom noshir shir
chodosh, uvirnonoh na-aleh,
horachamon hanikdosh, yisborach
v'yis-aleh, al kōs yayin
molay k'virkas adōnoy.

יִבָּנֶה הַמִּקְדָּשׁ, עִיר צִיּוֹן
תְּמַלֵּא, וְשָׁם נָשִׁיר שִׁיר
חָדָשׁ, וּבִרְנָנָה נַעֲלֶה,
הָרַחֲמָן הַנִּקְדָּשׁ, יִתְבָּרַךְ
וְיִתְעַלֶּה, עַל־כּוֹס יַיִן
מָלֵא כְּבִרְכַּת יְיָ.

Tzur mishelō ochalnu, borchu
emunai, sova-nu v'hōsarnu,
kidvar adōnoy.

צוּר מִשֶּׁלוֹ אָכַלְנוּ, בָּרְכוּ
אֱמוּנַי, שָׂבַעְנוּ וְהוֹתַרְנוּ,
כִּדְבַר יְיָ.

זְמִירוֹת לְיוֹם הַשַּׁבָּת
ZEMIROS FOR SHABBOS MORNING

7   *Boruch adōnoy yōm yōm*   בָּרוּךְ אֲדֹנָי יוֹם יוֹם

We bless the Lord for all He does for His people. Throughout our history—in Egypt, in Babylonia, in Persia and in all the countries of our exile—God has come to save us from the many tyrants who have oppressed us. May God gather us together once more as He promised. Blessed be God who has always been so good to us. Let us extol Him with all our might. May God bless Israel with peace so that we may be able to raise children who will occupy themselves with Torah and the commandments. God is the prince of peace.

Boruch adōnoy yōm yōm,	בָּרוּךְ אֲדֹנָי יוֹם יוֹם,
ya-amos lonu yesha ufidyōm,	יַעֲמָס־לָנוּ יֶשַׁע וּפִדְיוֹם,
uvishmō nogil kol ha-yōm,	וּבִשְׁמוֹ נָגִיל כָּל־הַיּוֹם,
uvishu-osō norim rōsh	וּבִישׁוּעָתוֹ נָרִים רֹאשׁ
elyōn, ki hu mo-ōz ladol	עֶלְיוֹן, כִּי הוּא מָעוֹז לַדָּל
umachseh lo-evyōn. Shivtay	וּמַחְסֶה לָאֶבְיוֹן. שִׁבְטֵי־
yoh l'yisro-ayl aydus,	יָהּ לְיִשְׂרָאֵל עֵדוּת,
b'tzorosom lō tzor b'sivlus	בְּצָרָתָם לוֹ צָר בְּסִבְלוּת
uv-avdus, b'livnas hasapir	וּבְעַבְדוּת, בְּלִבְנַת הַסַּפִּיר
her-om ōz y'didus, v'nigloh	הֶרְאָם עֹז יְדִידוּת, וְנִגְלָה
l'ha-alōsom may-ōmek bōr	לְהַעֲלוֹתָם מֵעֹמֶק בּוֹר
vodus, ki im adōnoy hachesed	וָדוּת, כִּי־עִם־יְיָ הַחֶסֶד
v'harbayh imō f'dus. Mah	וְהַרְבֵּה עִמּוֹ פְדוּת. מַה־
yokor chasdō b'tzilō l'gōn'naymō,	יָקָר חַסְדּוֹ בְּצִלּוֹ לְגוֹנְנֵמוֹ,
b'golus boveloh shulach	בְּגָלוּת בָּבֶלָה שֻׁלַּח
l'ma-anaymō, l'hōrid	לְמַעֲנֵמוֹ, לְהוֹרִיד
borichim nimnoh vaynaymō,	בָּרִיחִים נִמְנָה בֵּינֵימוֹ,
va-yitnaym l'rachamim lifnay	וַיִּתְּנֵם לְרַחֲמִים לִפְנֵי

37

shōvaymō, ki lō yitōsh adōnoy	שׁוֹבֵימוֹ, כִּי לֹא־יִטּשׁ יְיָ
es amō, ba-avur hagodōl	אֶת־עַמּוֹ, בַּעֲבוּר הַגָּדוֹל
sh'mō.	שְׁמוֹ.
Aylom shos kis-ō l'hatzil	עֵילָם שָׁת כִּסְאוֹ לְהַצִּיל
y'didov, l'ha-avir mishom	יְדִידָיו, לְהַעֲבִיר מִשָּׁם
mo-uznay mōrdov, may-avōr	מָאזְנֵי מוֹרְדָיו, מֵעֲבוֹר
bashelach podoh es avodov,	בַּשֶּׁלַח פָּדָה אֶת־עֲבָדָיו,
keren l'amō yorim t'hiloh	קֶרֶן לְעַמּוֹ יָרִים תְּהִלָּה
l'chol chasidov, ki im	לְכָל־חֲסִידָיו, כִּי אִם־
hōgoh v'richam k'rōv chasodov.	הוֹגָה וְרִחַם כְּרֹב חֲסָדָיו.
Utz'fir ho-izim higdil	וּצְפִיר הָעִזִּים הִגְדִּיל
atzumov, v'gam chozus arba	עֲצוּמָיו, וְגַם־חָזוּת אַרְבַּע
olu limrōmov, uvlibom	עָלוּ לִמְרוֹמָיו, וּבְלִבָּם
dimu l'hashchis es	דִּמּוּ לְהַשְׁחִית אֶת־
r'chumov, al y'day chōhanov	רְחוּמָיו, עַל־יְדֵי כֹהֲנָיו
migayr miskōm'mov, chasday adōnoy	מִגֵּר מִתְקוֹמְמָיו, חַסְדֵי יְיָ
ki lō somnu ki lō cholu	כִּי לֹא־תָמְנוּ כִּי לֹא־כָלוּ
rachamov. Nisgarti le-edōm	רַחֲמָיו. נִסְגַּרְתִּי לֶאֱדוֹם
b'yad ray-ai m'donai, shebchol	בְּיַד רֵעַי מְדָנַי, שֶׁבְּכָל־
yōm m'mal-im k'raysom	יוֹם מְמַלְּאִים כְּרֵסָם
may-adonai, ezrosō imi	מֵעֲדָנַי, עֶזְרָתוֹ עִמִּי
lismōch es adonai, v'lō	לִסְמֹךְ אֶת־אֲדָנַי, וְלֹא
n'tashtani kol y'may idonai, ki	נְטַשְׁתַּנִי כָּל־יְמֵי עֲדָנַי, כִּי
lō yiznach l'ōlom adōnoy.	לֹא יִזְנַח לְעוֹלָם אֲדָנָי.
B'vō-ō may-edōm chamutz	בְּבוֹאוֹ מֵאֱדוֹם חֲמוּץ
b'godim, zevach lō b'votzroh	בְּגָדִים, זֶבַח לוֹ בְּבָצְרָה
v'tevach lō b'vōgdim, v'yayz	וְטֶבַח לוֹ בְּבוֹגְדִים, וְיֵז
nitzchom malbushov	נִצְחָם מַלְבּוּשָׁיו

l'ha-dim, b'chōchō hagodōl	לְהָאדִים, בְּכֹחוֹ הַגָּדוֹל
yivtzōr ruach n'gidim, hogoh	יַבְצֹר רוּחַ נְגִידִים, הָגָה
b'ruchō hakoshoh b'yōm	בְּרוּחוֹ הַקָּשָׁה בְּיוֹם
kodim. R'ōsō ki chayn	קָדִים. רְאוֹתוֹ כִּי־כֵן
adōmi ho-ōtzayr, yachshov lō	אֲדֹמִי הָעוֹצֵר, יַחְשָׁב־לוֹ
botzroh tiklōt k'vetzer,	בָּצְרָה תִּקְלֹט כְּבֶצֶר,
umal-och k'odom b'sōchoh	וּמַלְאָךְ כְּאָדָם בְּתוֹכָהּ
yinotzayr, umayzid kashōgayg	יִנָּצֵר, וּמֵזִיד כַּשּׁוֹגֵג
b'miklot yay-otzayr, ehevu	בְּמִקְלָט יֵעָצֵר, אֶהֱבוּ
es adōnoy kol chasidov	אֶת־יְיָ כָּל־חֲסִידָיו
emunim nōtzayr. Y'tzaveh tzur	אֱמוּנִים נוֹצֵר. יְצַוֶּה צוּר
chasdō k'hilōsov l'kabaytz,	חַסְדּוֹ קְהִלּוֹתָיו לְקַבֵּץ,
may-arba ruchōs odov	מֵאַרְבַּע רוּחוֹת עָדָיו
l'hikovaytz, uvhar m'rōm	לְהִקָּבֵץ, וּבְהַר מְרוֹם־
horim ōsonu l'harbaytz,	הָרִים אוֹתָנוּ לְהַרְבֵּץ,
v'itonu yoshuv nidochim	וְאִתָּנוּ יָשׁוּב נִדָּחִים
kōvaytz, yoshiv lō ne-emar	קוֹבֵץ, יָשִׁיב לֹא נֶאֱמַר
ki im v'shov v'kibaytz.	כִּי־אִם וְשָׁב וְקִבֵּץ.
Boruch hu elōhaynu asher	בָּרוּךְ הוּא אֱלֹהֵינוּ אֲשֶׁר
tōv g'molonu, k'rachamov	טוֹב גְּמָלָנוּ, כְּרַחֲמָיו
uchrōv chasodov higdil lonu,	וּכְרֹב חֲסָדָיו הִגְדִּיל לָנוּ,
ayleh v'cho-ayleh yōsayf imonu,	אֵלֶּה וְכָאֵלֶּה יוֹסֵף עִמָּנוּ,
l'hagdil sh'mō hagodōl	לְהַגְדִּיל שְׁמוֹ הַגָּדוֹל
hagibōr v'hanōro shenikro	הַגִּבּוֹר וְהַנּוֹרָא שֶׁנִּקְרָא
olaynu. Boruch hu elōhaynu	עָלֵינוּ. בָּרוּךְ הוּא אֱלֹהֵינוּ
shebro-onu lichvōdō, l'hal'lō	שֶׁבְּרָאָנוּ לִכְבוֹדוֹ, לְהַלְלוֹ
ulshabchō ulsapayr hōdō,	וּלְשַׁבְּחוֹ וּלְסַפֵּר הוֹדוֹ,
mikol ōm govar olaynu	מִכָּל־אֹם גָּבַר עָלֵינוּ

chasdō, lochayn b'chol layv	חַסְדּוֹ, לָכֵן בְּכָל-לֵב
uvchol nefesh uvchol m'ōd	וּבְכָל-נֶפֶשׁ וּבְכָל-מְאוֹד
namlichō unyachadō. Shehasholōm	נַמְלִיכוֹ וּנְיַחֲדוֹ. שֶׁהַשָּׁלוֹם
shelō yosim olaynu b'rochoh	שֶׁלוֹ יָשִׂים עָלֵינוּ בְּרָכָה
v'sholōm, mismōl umiyomin	וְשָׁלוֹם, מִשְּׂמֹאל וּמִיָּמִין
al yisro-ayl sholōm,	עַל-יִשְׂרָאֵל שָׁלוֹם,
horachamon hu y'voraych	הָרַחֲמָן הוּא יְבָרֵךְ
es amō vasholōm, v'yizku	אֶת-עַמּוֹ בַשָּׁלוֹם, וְיִזְכּוּ
lir-ōs bonim	לִרְאוֹת בָּנִים
uvnay vonim ōskim	וּבְנֵי בָנִים עוֹסְקִים
batōrah uvmitzvōs,	בַּתּוֹרָה וּבְמִצְוֹת,
al yisro-ayl sholōm,	עַל-יִשְׂרָאֵל שָׁלוֹם,
yō-aytz ayl gibōr avi ad	יוֹעֵץ אֵל גִּבּוֹר אֲבִי-עַד
sar sholōm.	שַׂר-שָׁלוֹם.

8   Boruch ayl elyōn   בָּרוּךְ אֵל עֶלְיוֹן

Blessed is God who gives our weary souls rest. God told us to make Shabbos a special day and we will be amply rewarded for it. Remember to keep Shabbos holy; relax and enjoy its royal feeling. Let the Shabbos Queen bring blessing to your home.

Boruch ayl elyōn asher nosan	בָּרוּךְ אֵל עֶלְיוֹן אֲשֶׁר נָתַן
m'nuchoh, l'nafshaynu fidyōn	מְנוּחָה, לְנַפְשֵׁנוּ פִדְיוֹן
mishays va-anochoh, v'hu	מִשֵּׁאת וַאֲנָחָה, וְהוּא
yidrōsh l'tziyōn ir	יִדְרוֹשׁ לְצִיּוֹן עִיר
hanidochoh, ad onoh tugyōn	הַנִּדָּחָה, עַד-אָנָה תּוּגְיוֹן
nefesh ne-enochoh.	נֶפֶשׁ נֶאֱנָחָה.

Hashōmayr shabbos, habayn im	הַשּׁוֹמֵר שַׁבָּת, הַבֵּן עִם
habas, lo-ayl yayrotzu,	הַבַּת, לָאֵל יֵרָצוּ,
k'minchoh al machavas.	כְּמִנְחָה עַל-מַחֲבַת.

Rōchayv bo-arovōs melech	רוֹכֵב בָּעֲרָבוֹת מֶלֶךְ
ōlomim, es amō lishbōs	עוֹלָמִים, אֶת־עַמּוֹ לִשְׁבֹּת
izayn ban-imim, b'ma-acholōs	אִזֵּן בַּנְּעִימִים, בְּמַאֲכָלוֹת
arayvōs b'minay mat-amim,	עֲרֵבוֹת בְּמִינֵי מַטְעַמִּים,
b'malbushay chovōd	בְּמַלְבּוּשֵׁי כָבוֹד
zevach mishpochoh.	זֶבַח מִשְׁפָּחָה.
Hashōmayr shabbos, habayn im	הַשּׁוֹמֵר שַׁבָּת, הַבֵּן עִם
habas, lo-ayl yayrotzu,	הַבַּת, לָאֵל יֵרָצוּ,
k'minchoh al machavas.	כְּמִנְחָה עַל־מַחֲבַת.
V'ashray kol chōcheh	וְאַשְׁרֵי כָּל־חוֹכֶה
l'sashlumay chayfel, may-ays kōl	לְתַשְׁלוּמֵי כֵפֶל, מֵאֵת כֹּל
sōcheh shōchayn bo-arofel,	סוֹכֶה שׁוֹכֵן בָּעֲרָפֶל,
nachaloh lō yizkeh bohor	נַחֲלָה לוֹ יִזְכֶּה בָהָר
uvashofel, nachaloh umnuchoh	וּבַשָּׁפֶל, נַחֲלָה וּמְנוּחָה
kashemesh lō zorchoh.	כַּשֶּׁמֶשׁ לוֹ זָרְחָה.
Hashōmayr shabbos, habayn im	הַשּׁוֹמֵר שַׁבָּת, הַבֵּן עִם
habas, lo-ayl yayrotzu,	הַבַּת, לָאֵל יֵרָצוּ,
k'minchoh al machavas.	כְּמִנְחָה עַל־מַחֲבַת.
Kol shōmayr shabbos kados	כָּל־שׁוֹמֵר שַׁבָּת כַּדָּת
maychal'lō, hayn hachshayr chibas	מֵחַלְּלוֹ, הֵן הַכְשֵׁר חִבַּת
kōdesh gōrolō, v'im yaytzay	קֹדֶשׁ גּוֹרָלוֹ, וְאִם יֵצֵא
chōvas ha-yōm ashray lō,	חוֹבַת הַיּוֹם אַשְׁרֵי לוֹ,
l'ayl odōn m'chōl'lō	לָאֵל אָדוֹן מְחוֹלְלוֹ
minchoh hi sh'luchoh.	מִנְחָה הִיא שְׁלוּחָה.
Hashōmayr shabbos, habayn im	הַשּׁוֹמֵר שַׁבָּת, הַבֵּן עִם
habas, lo-ayl yayrotzu,	הַבַּת, לָאֵל יֵרָצוּ,
k'minchoh al machavas.	כְּמִנְחָה עַל־מַחֲבַת.

Chemdas ha-yomim k'ro-ō ayli	חֶמְדַּת הַיָּמִים קְרָאוֹ אֵלִי
tzur, v'ashray lismimim	צוּר, וְאַשְׁרֵי לִתְמִימִים
im yihyeh notzur, keser	אִם־יִהְיֶה נָצוּר, כֶּתֶר
hilumim al rōshom	הִלּוּמִים עַל־רֹאשָׁם
yotzur, tzur ho-ōlomim	יָצוּר, צוּר הָעוֹלָמִים
ruchō bom nochoh.	רוּחוֹ בָּם נָחָה.
Hashōmayr shabbos, habayn im	הַשׁוֹמֵר שַׁבָּת, הַבֵּן עִם
habas, lo-ayl yayrotzu,	הַבַּת, לָאֵל יֵרָצוּ,
k'minchoh al machavas.	כְּמִנְחָה עַל־מַחֲבַת.
Zochōr es yōm hashabbos	זָכוֹר אֶת־יוֹם הַשַּׁבָּת
l'kadshō, karnō ki govhoh	לְקַדְּשׁוֹ, קַרְנוֹ כִּי גָבְהָה
nayzer al rōshō, al kayn	נֵזֶר עַל־רֹאשׁוֹ, עַל־כֵּן
yitayn ho-odom l'nafshō, ōneg	יִתֵּן הָאָדָם לְנַפְשׁוֹ, עֹנֶג
v'gam simchoh bohem	וְגַם־שִׂמְחָה בָּהֶם
lō l'moshchoh.	לוֹ לְמָשְׁחָה.
Hashōmayr shabbos, habayn im	הַשׁוֹמֵר שַׁבָּת, הַבֵּן עִם
habas, lo-ayl yayrotzu,	הַבַּת, לָאֵל יֵרָצוּ,
k'minchoh al machavas.	כְּמִנְחָה עַל־מַחֲבַת.
Kōdesh hi lochem shabbos	קֹדֶשׁ הִיא לָכֶם שַׁבָּת
hamalkoh, el tōch botaychem	הַמַּלְכָּה, אֶל־תּוֹךְ בָּתֵּיכֶם
l'honiyach b'rochoh, b'chol	לְהָנִיחַ בְּרָכָה, בְּכָל־
mōshvōsaychem lō sa-asu	מוֹשְׁבוֹתֵיכֶם לֹא תַעֲשׂוּ
m'lochoh, b'naychem	מְלָאכָה, בְּנֵיכֶם
uvnōsaychem eved	וּבְנוֹתֵיכֶם עֶבֶד
v'gam shifchoh.	וְגַם־שִׁפְחָה.
Hashōmayr shabbos, habayn im	הַשׁוֹמֵר שַׁבָּת, הַבֵּן עִם
habas, lo-ayl yayrotzu,	הַבַּת, לָאֵל יֵרָצוּ,
k'minchoh al machavas.	כְּמִנְחָה עַל־מַחֲבַת.

This is the most precious of days because it is the day on which God rested. You should work for six days, but honor the seventh as Shabbos. Make kiddush, eat challah and other good things. When you are sated, bless God as He has blessed you. The whole universe attests to God's glory and perfection.

Yōm zeh m'chubod mikol yomim,	יוֹם זֶה מְכֻבָּד מִכָּל-יָמִים,
ki vō shovas tzur ōlomim.	כִּי בוֹ שָׁבַת צוּר עוֹלָמִים.
Shayshes yomim ta-aseh	שֵׁשֶׁת יָמִים תַּעֲשֶׂה
m'lach'techo, v'yōm hashvi-i	מְלַאכְתֶּךָ, וְיוֹם הַשְּׁבִיעִי
laylōhecho, shabbos lō	לֵאלֹהֶיךָ, שַׁבָּת לֹא
sa-aseh vō m'lochoh, ki	תַעֲשֶׂה בוֹ מְלָאכָה, כִּי
chōl osoh shayshes yomim.	כֹל עָשָׂה שֵׁשֶׁת יָמִים.
Yōm zeh m'chubod mikol yomim,	יוֹם זֶה מְכֻבָּד מִכָּל-יָמִים,
ki vō shovas tzur ōlomim.	כִּי בוֹ שָׁבַת צוּר עוֹלָמִים.
Rishōn hu l'mikro-ay	רִאשׁוֹן הוּא לְמִקְרָאֵי
kōdesh, yōm shabbosōn yōm	קֹדֶשׁ, יוֹם שַׁבָּתוֹן יוֹם
shabbas kōdesh, al kayn kol	שַׁבַּת קֹדֶשׁ, עַל כֵּן כָּל-
ish b'yaynō y'kadaysh, al	אִישׁ בְּיֵינוֹ יְקַדֵּשׁ, עַל
sh'tay lechem yivtz'u	שְׁתֵּי לֶחֶם יִבְצְעוּ
s'mimim.	תְמִימִים.
Yōm zeh m'chubod mikol yomim,	יוֹם זֶה מְכֻבָּד מִכָּל-יָמִים,
ki vō shovas tzur ōlomim.	כִּי בוֹ שָׁבַת צוּר עוֹלָמִים.
Echōl mashmanim sh'sayh	אֱכֹל מַשְׁמַנִּים שְׁתֵה
mamtakim, ki ayl yitayn	מַמְתַּקִים, כִּי אֵל יִתֵּן
l'chōl bō d'vaykim, beged	לְכֹל בּוֹ דְבֵקִים, בֶּגֶד
lilbōsh lechem chukim, bosor	לִלְבּוֹשׁ לֶחֶם חֻקִּים, בָּשָׂר
v'dogim v'chol mat-amim.	וְדָגִים וְכָל-מַטְעַמִּים.

Yōm zeh m'chubod mikol yomim,	יוֹם זֶה מְכֻבָּד מִכָּל־יָמִים,
ki vō shovas tzur ōlomim.	כִּי בוֹ שָׁבַת צוּר עוֹלָמִים.
Lō sechsar kōl bō v'ochalto,	לֹא תֶחְסַר כֹּל בּוֹ וְאָכַלְתָּ,
v'sovo-to uvayrachto,	וְשָׂבַעְתָּ וּבֵרַכְתָּ,
es adōnoy elōhecho asher	אֶת־יְיָ אֱלֹהֶיךָ אֲשֶׁר
ohavto, ki vayrach'cho	אָהַבְתָּ, כִּי בֵרַכְךָ
mikol ho-amim.	מִכָּל־הָעַמִּים.
Yōm zeh m'chubod mikol yomim,	יוֹם זֶה מְכֻבָּד מִכָּל־יָמִים,
ki vō shovas tzur ōlomim.	כִּי בוֹ שָׁבַת צוּר עוֹלָמִים.
Hashoma-yim m'saprim k'vōdō,	הַשָּׁמַיִם מְסַפְּרִים כְּבוֹדוֹ,
v'gam ho-oretz mol-oh chasdō,	וְגַם־הָאָרֶץ מָלְאָה חַסְדּוֹ,
r'u ki chol ayleh os'soh	רְאוּ כִּי כָל־אֵלֶּה עָשְׂתָה
yodō, ki hu hatzur	יָדוֹ, כִּי הוּא הַצּוּר
po-olō somim.	פָּעֳלוֹ תָמִים.
Yōm zeh m'chubod mikol yomim,	יוֹם זֶה מְכֻבָּד מִכָּל־יָמִים,
ki vō shovas tzur ōlomim.	כִּי בוֹ שָׁבַת צוּר עוֹלָמִים.

10 Yōm shabbosōn — יוֹם שַׁבָּתוֹן

Shabbos is a day of rest which we are all careful to honor. Israel has a covenant with God in which He told us to rest on Shabbos. We will keep our side of the agreement and look to God to keep His—to see that no harm befalls us.

Yōm shabbosōn ayn lishkōach,	יוֹם שַׁבָּתוֹן אֵין לִשְׁכֹּחַ,
zichrō k'rayach hanichōach. Yōnoh	זִכְרוֹ כְּרֵיחַ הַנִּיחֹחַ. יוֹנָה
motz-oh bō monōach, v'shom	מָצְאָה בוֹ מָנוֹחַ, וְשָׁם
yonuchu y'gi-ay chōach.	יָנוּחוּ יְגִיעֵי כֹחַ.

44

Ha-yōm nichbod livnay emunim,	הַיּוֹם נִכְבָּד לִבְנֵי אֱמוּנִים,
z'hirim l'shomrō ovōs	זְהִירִים לְשָׁמְרוֹ אָבוֹת
uvonim, chokuk bishnay luchōs	וּבָנִים, חָקוּק בִּשְׁנֵי לֻחוֹת
avonim, mayrōv ōnim	אֲבָנִים, מֵרוֹב אוֹנִים
v'amitz kōach.	וְאַמִּיץ כֹּחַ.
Yōnoh motz-oh bō monōach,	יוֹנָה מָצְאָה בוֹ מָנוֹחַ,
v'shom yonuchu y'gi-ay chōach.	וְשָׁם יָנוּחוּ יְגִיעֵי כֹחַ.
Uvo-u chulom bivris yachad,	וּבָאוּ כֻלָּם בִּבְרִית יַחַד,
na-aseh v'nishma omru	נַעֲשֶׂה וְנִשְׁמַע אָמְרוּ
k'echod, ufos-chu v'onu adōnoy	כְּאֶחָד, וּפָתְחוּ וְעָנוּ יְיָ
echod, boruch hanōsayn	אֶחָד, בָּרוּךְ הַנּוֹתֵן
la-yo-ayf kōach.	לַיָּעֵף כֹּחַ.
Yōnoh motz-oh bō monōach,	יוֹנָה מָצְאָה בוֹ מָנוֹחַ,
v'shom yonuchu y'gi-ay chōach.	וְשָׁם יָנוּחוּ יְגִיעֵי כֹחַ.
Diber b'kodshō b'har hamōr,	דִּבֶּר בְּקָדְשׁוֹ בְּהַר הַמֹּר,
yōm hashvi-i zochōr	יוֹם הַשְּׁבִיעִי זָכוֹר
v'shomōr, v'chol pikudov yachad	וְשָׁמוֹר, וְכָל־פִּקוּדָיו יַחַד
ligmōr, chazayk mosna-yim	לִגְמוֹר, חַזֵּק מָתְנַיִם
v'amaytz kōach.	וְאַמֵּץ כֹּחַ.
Yōnoh motz-oh bō monōach,	יוֹנָה מָצְאָה בוֹ מָנוֹחַ,
v'shom yonuchu y'gi-ay chōach.	וְשָׁם יָנוּחוּ יְגִיעֵי כֹחַ.
Ho-om asher no katzōn	הָעָם אֲשֶׁר נָע כַּצֹּאן
to-oh, yizkōr l'fokdō b'ris	תָּעָה, יִזְכֹּר לְפָקְדוֹ בְּרִית
ushvu-oh, l'val ya-avor bom	וּשְׁבוּעָה, לְבַל יַעֲבָר־בָּם
mikrayh ro-oh, ka-asher	מִקְרֵה רָעָה, כַּאֲשֶׁר
nishba al may nōach.	נִשְׁבַּע עַל־מֵי נֹחַ.
Yōnoh motz-oh bō monōach,	יוֹנָה מָצְאָה בוֹ מָנוֹחַ,
v'shom yonuchu y'gi-ay chōach.	וְשָׁם יָנוּחוּ יְגִיעֵי כֹחַ.

11   *Ki eshm'roh shabbos*   כִּי אֶשְׁמְרָה שַׁבָּת

If we observe Shabbos, God will watch over us. It is not a day for pursuing our regular occupation, or even discussing it; rather it is for Torah study. Just as a double portion of mannah fell on Friday, so may God double our portion. We must eat challah; we may not fast on Shabbos except on Yom Kippur. It is a day for good food and good feelings, a day to pray to God in the knowledge that He will answer.

Ki eshm'roh shabbos ayl   כִּי אֶשְׁמְרָה שַׁבָּת אֵל
yishm'rayni, ōs hi   יִשְׁמְרֵנִי, אוֹת הִיא
l'ōlmay ad baynō uvayni.   לְעוֹלְמֵי עַד בֵּינוֹ וּבֵינִי.

Osur m'tzō chafetz asōs   אָסוּר מְצֹא חֵפֶץ עֲשׂוֹת
d'rochim, gam mildabayr bō   דְּרָכִים, גַּם מִלְּדַבֵּר בּוֹ
divray tz'rochim, divray   דִּבְרֵי צְרָכִים, דִּבְרֵי
s'chōroh af divray m'lochim,   סְחוֹרָה אַף דִּבְרֵי מְלָכִים,
ehgeh b'sōras ayl   אֶהְגֶּה בְּתוֹרַת אֵל
us-chakmayni.   וּתְחַכְּמֵנִי.

Ki eshm'roh shabbos ayl   כִּי אֶשְׁמְרָה שַׁבָּת אֵל
yishm'rayni, ōs hi   יִשְׁמְרֵנִי, אוֹת הִיא
l'ōlmay ad baynō uvayni.   לְעוֹלְמֵי עַד בֵּינוֹ וּבֵינִי.

Bō emtzo somid nōfesh   בּוֹ אֶמְצָא תָּמִיד נֹפֶשׁ
l'nafshi, hinayh l'dōr   לְנַפְשִׁי, הִנֵּה לְדוֹר
rishōn nosan k'dōshi, mōfays   רִאשׁוֹן נָתַן קְדוֹשִׁי, מוֹפֵת
b'says lechem mishneh bashishi,   בְּתֵת לֶחֶם מִשְׁנֶה בַּשִּׁשִּׁי,
kochoh v'chol shishi   כָּכָה בְּכָל־שִׁשִּׁי
yachpil m'zōni.   יַכְפִּיל מְזוֹנִי.

Ki eshm'roh shabbos ayl   כִּי אֶשְׁמְרָה שַׁבָּת אֵל
yishm'rayni, ōs hi   יִשְׁמְרֵנִי, אוֹת הִיא
l'ōlmay ad baynō uvayni.   לְעוֹלְמֵי עַד בֵּינוֹ וּבֵינִי.

Rosham b'das ho-ayl chōk el s'gonov, bō la-arōch lechem ponim b'fonov, al kayn l'his-anōs bō al pi n'vōnov, osur l'vad miyōm kipur aūni.	רָשַׁם בְּדַת הָאֵל חֹק אֶל- סְגָנָיו, בּוֹ לַעֲרוֹךְ לֶחֶם פָּנִים בְּפָנָיו, עַל-כֵּן לְהִתְעַנּוֹת בּוֹ עַל-פִּי נְבוֹנָיו, אָסוּר לְבַד מִיּוֹם כִּפּוּר עֲוֹנִי.
Ki eshm'roh shabbos ayl yishm'rayni, ōs hi l'ōlmay ad baynō uvayni.	כִּי אֶשְׁמְרָה שַׁבָּת אֵל יִשְׁמְרֵנִי, אוֹת הִיא לְעוֹלְמֵי עַד בֵּינוֹ וּבֵינִי.
Hu yōm m'chubod hu yōm ta-anugim, lechem v'ya-yin tōv bosor v'dogim, hamis-ablim bō ochōr n'sōgim, ki yōm s'mochōs hu us'samchayni.	הוּא יוֹם מְכֻבָּד הוּא יוֹם תַּעֲנוּגִים, לֶחֶם וְיַיִן טוֹב בָּשָׂר וְדָגִים, הַמִּתְאַבְּלִים בּוֹ אָחוֹר נְסוֹגִים, כִּי יוֹם שְׂמָחוֹת הוּא וּתְשַׂמְּחֵנִי.
Ki eshm'roh shabbos ayl yishm'rayni, ōs hi l'ōlmay ad baynō uvayni.	כִּי אֶשְׁמְרָה שַׁבָּת אֵל יִשְׁמְרֵנִי, אוֹת הִיא לְעוֹלְמֵי עַד בֵּינוֹ וּבֵינִי.
Maychayl m'lochoh bō sōfō l'hachris, al kayn achabays bō libi k'vōris, v'espal'loh el ayl arvis v'shacharis, musof v'gam minchoh hu ya-anayni.	מֵחֵל מְלָאכָה בּוֹ סוֹפוֹ לְהַכְרִית, עַל-כֵּן אֲכַבֶּס- בּוֹ לִבִּי כְּבוֹרִית, וְאֶתְפַּלְלָה אֶל-אֵל עַרְבִית וְשַׁחֲרִית, מוּסָף וְגַם-מִנְחָה הוּא יַעֲנֵנִי.
Ki eshm'roh shabbos ayl yishm'rayni, ōs hi l'ōlmay ad baynō uvayni.	כִּי אֶשְׁמְרָה שַׁבָּת אֵל יִשְׁמְרֵנִי, אוֹת הִיא לְעוֹלְמֵי עַד בֵּינוֹ וּבֵינִי.

God provides protection for us: praise Him unceasingly and keep Shabbos.
May God restore the Temple and answer the prayer of His people. May He
stamp on our enemies and send the redeemer. May He grant peace to those
who keep Shabbos.

D'rōr yikro l'vayn im bas,	דְּרוֹר יִקְרָא לְבֵן עִם בַּת,
v'yintzorchem k'mō vovas,	וְיִנְצָרְכֶם כְּמוֹ בָבַת,
n'im shimchem v'lō yushbas,	נְעִים שִׁמְכֶם וְלֹא יֻשְׁבַּת,
sh'vu v'nuchu b'yōm shabbos.	שְׁבוּ וְנוּחוּ בְּיוֹם שַׁבָּת.

D'rōsh novi v'ulami,	דְּרוֹשׁ נָוִי וְאוּלְמִי,
v'ōs yesha asayh imi,	וְאוֹת יֵשַׁע עֲשֵׂה עִמִּי,
n'ta sōrayk b'sōch karmi,	נְטַע שׂוֹרֵק בְּתוֹךְ כַּרְמִי,
sh'ayh shav-as b'nay ami.	שְׁעֵה שַׁוְעַת בְּנֵי עַמִּי.

D'rōch puroh b'sōch botzroh,	דְּרוֹךְ פּוּרָה בְּתוֹךְ בָּצְרָה,
v'gam bovel asher govroh,	וְגַם־בָּבֶל אֲשֶׁר גָּבְרָה,
n'sōtz tzorai b'af v'evroh,	נְתוֹץ צָרַי בְּאַף וְעֶבְרָה,
sh'ma kōli b'yōm ekro.	שְׁמַע קוֹלִי בְּיוֹם אֶקְרָא.

Elōhim tayn b'midbor har,	אֱלֹהִים תֵּן בְּמִדְבָּר הַר,
hadas shitoh b'rōsh tidhor,	הֲדַס שִׁטָּה בְּרוֹשׁ תִּדְהָר,
v'lamazhir v'lanizhor,	וְלַמַּזְהִיר וְלַנִּזְהָר,
sh'lōmim tayn k'may nohor.	שְׁלוֹמִים תֵּן כְּמֵי נָהָר.

Hadōch komai ayl kano,	הֲדוֹךְ קָמַי אֵל קַנָּא,
b'mōg layvov uvamginoh,	בְּמוֹג לֵבָב וּבַמְּגִנָּה,
v'narchiv peh unmal-enoh,	וְנַרְחִיב פֶּה וּנְמַלְאֶנָּה,
l'shōnaynu l'cho rinoh.	לְשׁוֹנֵנוּ לְךָ רִנָּה.

D'ayh chochmoh l'nafshecho,	דְּעֵה חָכְמָה לְנַפְשֶׁךָ,
v'hi cheser l'rōshecho,	וְהִיא כֶתֶר לְרֹאשֶׁךָ,
n'tzōr mitzvas k'dōshecho,	נְצוֹר מִצְוַת קְדוֹשֶׁךָ,
sh'mōr shabbas kodshecho.	שְׁמוֹר שַׁבַּת קָדְשֶׁךָ.

זְמִירוֹת לִסְעוּדָה שְׁלִישִׁית
ZEMIROS FOR THE THIRD MEAL

13 B'nay Haycholo   בְּנֵי הֵיכָלָא

May the Eternal Holy One join us at Minchah time, when He is especially
well-disposed towards us and will show no anger. As He banishes all evil and
harmful influences, we will be filled with joy.

Askinu s'udoso	אַתְקִינוּ סְעוּדָתָא
dimhaym'nuso, sh'laymoso	דִּמְהֵימְנוּתָא, שְׁלֵימָתָא
chedvoso d'malko kadisho,	חֶדְוָתָא דְּמַלְכָּא קַדִּישָׁא,
askinu s'udoso d'malko.	אַתְקִינוּ סְעוּדָתָא דְּמַלְכָּא.
Do hi s'udoso diz-ayr	דָּא הִיא סְעוּדָתָא דִּזְעֵיר
anpin v'atiko kadisho	אַנְפִּין וְעַתִּיקָא קַדִּישָׁא
vachakal tapuchin kadishin	וַחֲקַל תַּפּוּחִין קַדִּישִׁין
asyon l'sa-ado bahadayh.	אַתְיָן לְסַעֲדָא בַּהֲדֵהּ.
B'nay haycholo, dichsifin,	בְּנֵי הֵיכָלָא, דִּכְסִיפִין,
l'mechezay ziv diz-ayr anpin.	לְמֶחֱזֵי זִיו דִּזְעֵיר אַנְפִּין.
Y'hōn hocho, b'hai tako,	יְהוֹן הָכָא, בְּהַאי תַּכָּא,
d'vayh malko b'gilufin.	דְּבֵהּ מַלְכָּא בְּגִלּוּפִין.

49

Tz'vu lachado, b'hai va-ado,	צְבוּ לַחֲדָא, בְּהַאי וַעֲדָא,
b'gō irin v'chol gadfin.	בְּגוֹ עִירִין וְכָל־גַּדְפִין.
Chadu hashto, b'hai sha-to,	חֲדוּ הַשְׁתָּא, בְּהַאי שַׁעְתָּא,
d'vayh ra-avo v'lays za-afin.	דְּבֵהּ רַעֲוָא וְלֵית זַעֲפִין.
K'rivu li, chazu chayli,	קְרִיבוּ לִי, חֲזוּ חֵילִי,
d'lays dinin diskifin.	דְּלֵית דִּינִין דִּתְקִיפִין.
L'var natlin, v'lo olin,	לְבַר נַטְלִין, וְלָא עָאלִין,
hanay chalbin dachatzifin.	הֲנֵי כַלְבִּין דַּחֲצִיפִין.
V'ho azmin, atik yōmin,	וְהָא אַזְמִין, עַתִּיק יוֹמִין,
l'minchoh (l'mitzcho)	לְמִנְחָה (לְמִצְחָא)
aday y'hōn cholfin.	עֲדֵי יְהוֹן חָלְפִין.
R'u dilayh, d'galay layh,	רְעוּ דִילֵהּ, דְּגַלֵי לֵהּ,
l'vatolo b'chol k'lifin.	לְבַטָּלָא בְּכָל־קְלִיפִין.
Y'shavay lōn, b'nōkvayhōn,	יְשַׁוֵּי לוֹן, בְּנוֹקְבֵּיהוֹן,
vitamrun b'gō chayfin.	וְיִטַּמְרוּן בְּגוֹ כֵּפִין.
Aray hashto, b'minchoso,	אֲרֵי הַשְׁתָּא, בְּמִנְחָתָא,
b'chedvoso diz-ayr anpin.	בְּחֶדְוָתָא דִּזְעֵיר אַנְפִּין.

14 Mizmōr l'dovid — מִזְמוֹר לְדָוִד

Mizmōr l'dovid. Adōnoy rō-i, lō	מִזְמוֹר לְדָוִד. יְיָ רֹעִי, לֹא
echsor. Bin-ōs deshe	אֶחְסָר. בִּנְאוֹת דֶּשֶׁא
yarbitzayni, al may m'nuchōs	יַרְבִּיצֵנִי, עַל מֵי מְנוּחוֹת
y'nahalayni. Nafshi y'shōvayv,	יְנַהֲלֵנִי. נַפְשִׁי יְשׁוֹבֵב,
yanchayni v'ma-g'lay tzedek l'ma-an	יַנְחֵנִי בְמַעְגְּלֵי צֶדֶק לְמַעַן
sh'mō. Gam ki aylaych b'gay	שְׁמוֹ. גַּם כִּי אֵלֵךְ בְּגֵיא
tzalmoves lō iro ro, ki	צַלְמָוֶת לֹא אִירָא רָע, כִּי
atoh imodi, shivt'cho	אַתָּה עִמָּדִי, שִׁבְטְךָ
umish-antecho, haymoh y'nachamuni.	וּמִשְׁעַנְתֶּךָ, הֵמָּה יְנַחֲמֻנִי.

Ta-arōch l'fonai shulchon, neged	תַּעֲרֹךְ לְפָנַי שֻׁלְחָן, נֶגֶד
tzōr'roy, dishanto vashemen	צֹרְרָי, דִּשַּׁנְתָּ בַשֶּׁמֶן
rōshi, kōsi r'voyoh. Ach	רֹאשִׁי, כּוֹסִי רְוָיָה. אַךְ
tōv vochesed yird'funi	טוֹב וָחֶסֶד יִרְדְּפוּנִי
kol y'may cha-yoy, v'shavti	כָּל-יְמֵי חַיָּי, וְשַׁבְתִּי
b'vays adōnoy l'ōrecho yomim.	בְּבֵית יְיָ לְאֹרֶךְ יָמִים.

A psalm of David. The Lord is my shepherd; I shall not want. He makes me lie down in green pastures; He leads me past still waters. He restores my soul; He leads me in the paths of righteousness, for His name's sake. Even though I walk in the valley of the shadow of death, I will fear no evil for You are with me. Your rod and Your staff—they comfort me. You set a table before me in the presence of my enemies. You have scented my head with oil; my cup overflows. Surely goodness and mercy will follow me all the days of my life and I will dwell in the house of the Lord forever.

15 Y'did nefesh   יְדִיד נֶפֶשׁ

Y'did nefesh ov horachamon	יְדִיד נֶפֶשׁ אָב הָרַחֲמָן
m'shōch avdecho el r'tzōnecho,	מְשׁוֹךְ עַבְדְּךָ אֶל רְצוֹנֶךָ,
yorutz avdecho k'mō a-yol,	יָרוּץ עַבְדְּךָ כְּמוֹ אַיָּל,
yishtachaveh el mul hadorecho,	יִשְׁתַּחֲוֶה אֶל מוּל הֲדָרֶךָ,
ye-erav lō y'didōsecho, minōfes	יֶעֱרַב לוֹ יְדִידוֹתֶךָ, מִנֹּפֶת
tzuf v'chol to-am.	צוּף וְכָל-טָעַם.

Hodur no-eh ziv ho-ōlom,	הָדוּר נָאֶה זִיו הָעוֹלָם,
nafshi chōlas ahavosecho,	נַפְשִׁי חוֹלַת אַהֲבָתֶךָ,
ono ayl no r'fo no loh,	אָנָּא אֵל נָא רְפָא נָא לָהּ,
b'har-ōs loh nō-am zivoch,	בְּהַרְאוֹת לָהּ נֹעַם זִיוֶךָ,
oz tis-chazayk v'sisrapay,	אָז תִּתְחַזֵּק וְתִתְרַפֵּא,
v'hoysoh loh	וְהָיְתָה לָהּ
simchas ōlom.	שִׂמְחַת עוֹלָם.

51

Vosik yehemu no rachamecho,	וָתִיק יֶהֱמוּ נָא רַחֲמֶיךָ,
v'chusoh no al bayn ahuvecho,	וְחוּסָה נָא עַל בֵּן אֲהוּבֶךָ,
ki zeh kamoh nichsōf	כִּי זֶה כַּמָּה נִכְסֹף
nichsafti, lir-ōs	נִכְסַפְתִּי, לִרְאוֹת
b'sif-eres uzecho, ayleh	בְּתִפְאֶרֶת עֻזֶּךָ, אֵלֶּה
chomdoh libi, v'chusoh no	חָמְדָה לִבִּי, וְחוּסָה נָא
v'al tis-alom.	וְאַל תִּתְעַלָּם.
Higoleh no ufrōs chavivi	הִגָּלֵה נָא וּפְרוֹשׂ חֲבִיבִי
olai, es sukas sh'lōmecho,	עָלַי, אֶת־סֻכַּת שְׁלוֹמֶךָ,
to-ir eretz mikvōdecho,	תָּאִיר אֶרֶץ מִכְּבוֹדֶךָ,
nogiloh v'nism'choh voch, mahayr	נָגִילָה וְנִשְׂמְחָה בָךְ, מַהֵר
ehōv ki vo mō-ayd,	אֱהוֹב כִּי בָא מוֹעֵד,
v'chonaynu kimay ōlom.	וְחָנֵּנוּ כִּימֵי עוֹלָם.

Beloved of my soul, merciful father, draw Your servant towards You. Let Your servant run as a hind to bow before Your glory. Let Your affection for him be sweeter than a honeycomb or any other delicacy.

Glorious one, most beautiful splendor of the world, my soul is sick with love for You. Please God, heal it by revealing the delight of Your splendor. Then it will be invigorated and healed, enjoying everlasting happiness.

Ancient one, let Your mercy be aroused and have pity on Your beloved son. For I have yearned for so long to see Your mighty splendor. This is the desire of my heart—have pity and do not hide Yourself.

Reveal Yourself and spread over me, beloved one, the shelter of Your peace. Let the earth sparkle with Your glory; we will rejoice and be happy with You. Be quick, beloved, for the time has come, and favor us as in days of old.

הַבְדָּלָה
HAVDOLOH

At the close of Shabbos, Havdoloh is recited over a brimming cup of wine,
sweet-smelling spices and a multi-wick candle. At the close of a festival on a
weekday evening, omit the first paragraph, the spices and the candle.

Hinayh ayl y'shu-osi, evtach	הִנֵּה אֵל יְשׁוּעָתִי, אֶבְטַח
v'lō efchod, ki ozi	וְלֹא אֶפְחָד, כִּי עָזִּי
v'zimros yoh adōnoy, vai-hi li	וְזִמְרָת יָהּ יְיָ, וַיְהִי לִי
lishu-oh. Ush'avtem ma-yim	לִישׁוּעָה. וּשְׁאַבְתֶּם מַיִם
b'sosōn mima-ai-nay hai-shu-oh.	בְּשָׂשׂוֹן מִמַּעַיְנֵי הַיְשׁוּעָה.
Ladōnoy hai-shu-oh, al amcho	לַיְיָ הַיְשׁוּעָה, עַל עַמְּךָ
birchosecho seloh. Adonoy tz'vo-ōs	בִרְכָתֶךָ סֶּלָה. יְיָ צְבָאוֹת
imonu, misgav lonu elōhay	עִמָּנוּ, מִשְׂגָּב לָנוּ אֱלֹהֵי
ya-akōv seloh. Adonoy tz'vo-ōs,	יַעֲקֹב סֶלָה. יְיָ צְבָאוֹת,
ashray odom bōtayach boch, adōnoy,	אַשְׁרֵי אָדָם בֹּטֵחַ בָּךְ, יְיָ,
hōshi-oh, hamelech ya-anaynu	הוֹשִׁיעָה, הַמֶּלֶךְ יַעֲנֵנוּ
v'yōm kor-aynu. Lai-hudim	בְיוֹם קָרְאֵנוּ. לַיְּהוּדִים
hoysoh ōroh v'simchoh,	הָיְתָה אוֹרָה וְשִׂמְחָה,
v'sosōn vikor. Kayn tihyeh	וְשָׂשׂוֹן וִיקָר. כֵּן תִּהְיֶה
lonu. Kōs y'shu-ōs eso,	לָנוּ. כּוֹס יְשׁוּעוֹת אֶשָּׂא,
uvshaym adōnoy ekro.	וּבְשֵׁם יְיָ אֶקְרָא.

Behold God is my salvation, I will have trust and not be afraid. Indeed, the
Lord is my strength and my song and He has become my salvation. You shall
draw water with joy from the wells of salvation. Salvation belongs to the
Lord; may Your blessings be upon Your people, Selah. The Lord of Hosts is
with us, the God of Jacob is a refuge for us, Selah. Lord of Hosts, happy is
the man who trusts in You. Lord, save us; may the king answer us on the
day we call. "The Jews had radiance and happiness, joy and honor"—so may
it be for us. I will lift up the cup of salvation and call on the name of the
Lord.

Sovray moronon v'rabonon v'rabōsai:　　　סָבְרֵי מָרָנָן וְרַבָּנָן וְרַבּוֹתַי:

For the wine:

Boruch atoh adōnoy,　　　בָּרוּךְ אַתָּה יְיָ,

elōhaynu melech ho-ōlom,　　　אֱלֹהֵינוּ מֶלֶךְ הָעוֹלָם,

bōray p'ri hagofen.　　　בּוֹרֵא פְּרִי הַגָּפֶן.

You are blessed, Lord our God, the sovereign of the world, creator of the fruit of the vine.

For the spices:

Boruch atoh adōnoy,　　　בָּרוּךְ אַתָּה יְיָ,

elōhaynu melech ho-ōlom,　　　אֱלֹהֵינוּ מֶלֶךְ הָעוֹלָם,

bōray minay v'somim.　　　בּוֹרֵא מִינֵי בְשָׂמִים.

You are blessed, Lord our God, the sovereign of the world, creator of various kinds of spices.

For the flames:

Boruch atoh adōnoy,　　　בָּרוּךְ אַתָּה יְיָ,

elōhaynu melech ho-ōlom,　　　אֱלֹהֵינוּ מֶלֶךְ הָעוֹלָם,

bōray m'ōray ho-aysh.　　　בּוֹרֵא מְאוֹרֵי הָאֵשׁ.

You are blessed, Lord our God, the sovereign of the world, creator of the lights of fire.

Boruch atoh adōnoy,　　　בָּרוּךְ אַתָּה יְיָ,

elōhaynu melech ho-ōlom,　　　אֱלֹהֵינוּ מֶלֶךְ הָעוֹלָם,

hamavdil bayn kōdesh l'chōl,　　　הַמַּבְדִּיל בֵּין קֹדֶשׁ לְחֹל,

bayn ōr l'chōshech, bayn　　　בֵּין אוֹר לְחֹשֶׁךְ, בֵּין

yisro-ayl lo-amim, bayn　　　יִשְׂרָאֵל לָעַמִּים, בֵּין

yōm hashvi-i l'shayshes　　　יוֹם הַשְּׁבִיעִי לְשֵׁשֶׁת

y'may hama-aseh.　　　יְמֵי הַמַּעֲשֶׂה.

Boruch atoh adōnoy,　　　בָּרוּךְ אַתָּה יְיָ,

hamavdil bayn kōdesh l'chōl.　　　הַמַּבְדִּיל בֵּין קֹדֶשׁ לְחֹל.

You are blessed, Lord our God, the sovereign of the world, who makes a distinction between sacred and secular, between light and darkness, between Israel and the other nations, between the seventh day and the six working days. You are blessed, Lord, who makes a distinction between the sacred and the secular.

הַמַּבְדִּיל

Hamavdil

Hamavdil bayn kōdesh l'chōl,	הַמַּבְדִּיל בֵּין קֹדֶשׁ לְחֹל,
chatōsaynu hu yimchōl,	חַטֹּאתֵינוּ הוּא יִמְחֹל,
zar-aynu v'chaspaynu yarbeh	זַרְעֵנוּ וְכַסְפֵּנוּ יַרְבֶּה
kachōl, v'chakōchovim baloyloh.	כַּחוֹל, וְכַכּוֹכָבִים בַּלָּיְלָה.
Yōm ponoh k'tzayl tōmer,	יוֹם פָּנָה כְּצֵל תֹּמֶר,
ekro lo-ayl olai gōmayr,	אֶקְרָא לָאֵל עָלַי גֹּמֵר,
omar shōmayr, oso vōker,	אָמַר שֹׁמֵר, אָתָא בֹקֶר,
v'gam loyloh.	וְגַם לָיְלָה.
Tzidkos-cho k'har tovōr,	צִדְקָתְךָ כְּהַר תָּבוֹר,
al chato-ai ovōr ta-avōr,	עַל חֲטָאַי עָבֹר תַּעֲבֹר,
k'yōm esmōl ki ya-avōr,	כְּיוֹם אֶתְמוֹל כִּי יַעֲבֹר,
v'ashmuroh valoyloh.	וְאַשְׁמוּרָה בַלָּיְלָה.
Cholfoh ōnas minchosi,	חָלְפָה עוֹנַת מִנְחָתִי,
mi yitayn m'nuchosi,	מִי יִתֵּן מְנוּחָתִי,
yoga-ti v'anchosi,	יָגַעְתִּי בְאַנְחָתִי,
as-cheh v'chol loyloh.	אַשְׂחֶה בְכָל לָיְלָה.
Kōli bal yutal,	קוֹלִי בַּל יֻטַּל,
p'sach li sha-ar hamnutol,	פְּתַח לִי שַׁעַר הַמְנֻטָּל,
sherōshi nimlo tol,	שֶׁרֹאשִׁי נִמְלָא טָל,
k'vutzōsai r'sisay loyloh.	קְוֻצּוֹתַי רְסִיסֵי לָיְלָה.
Hay-osayr nōro v'oyōm,	הֵעָתֵר נוֹרָא וְאָיֹם,
ashavay-a t'noh fidyōm,	אֲשַׁוֵּעַ תְּנָה פִדְיוֹם,

b'neshef b'erev yōm,	בְּנֶשֶׁף בְּעֶרֶב יוֹם,
b'ishōn loyloh.	בְּאִישׁוֹן לָיְלָה.
K'rosicho yoh hōshi-ayni,	קְרָאתִיךָ יָהּ הוֹשִׁיעֵנִי,
ōrach chayim tōdi-ayni,	אֹרַח חַיִּים תּוֹדִיעֵנִי,
midaloh s'vatz-ayni,	מִדַּלָּה תְבַצְּעֵנִי,
miyōm ad loyloh.	מִיּוֹם עַד לָיְלָה.
Tahayr tinuf ma-asai,	טַהֵר טִנּוּף מַעֲשַׂי,
pen yōm'ru mach-isai,	פֶּן יֹאמְרוּ מַכְעִיסָי,
ayayh elōah ōsoy,	אַיֵּה אֱלוֹהַּ עֹשָׂי,
hanōsayn z'mirōs baloyloh.	הַנֹּתֵן זְמִרוֹת בַּלָּיְלָה.
Nachnu v'yodcho kachōmer,	נַחְנוּ בְיָדְךָ כַּחֹמֶר,
s'lach no al kal vochōmer,	סְלַח נָא עַל קַל וָחֹמֶר,
yōm l'yōm yabi-a ōmer,	יוֹם לְיוֹם יַבִּיעַ אֹמֶר,
v'lailoh l'loyloh.	וְלַיְלָה לְלָיְלָה.

He who makes a distinction between the sacred and the secular, may He also pardon our sins. May He proliferate our children and our wealth like the sand, and like the stars at night.

Twilight has arrived like the shade of a palm tree; I call to God who gives me everything. The watchman says morning comes, but night, too.

Your righteousness is as great as Mount Tabor; please ignore, disregard my sins. May they be like yesterday—gone—like a watch in the night.

The time when I would bring offerings is long gone. If only I had rest! I am so tired of sighing, I weep every night.

Do not allow my voice to be stifled; open the gate on high for me; for my head is soaked with dew, my locks with the drops of the night.

Grant my prayer, revered and awesome one; I implore You, bring redemption, at dusk, in the evening, in the dark of night.

I am calling You, God, save me; show me life's scheme. Keep me from poverty, by day and by night.

Purify the defilement of my actions, lest those who incite me ask where is the God who made me, who can inspire hymns in the night.

We are as clay in Your hand; please forgive our petty and our major sins. Each day tells the story, and each night.

סדר ברכות

Blessings

בִּרְכַּת הַמָּזוֹן
THE BLESSING AFTER THE MEAL

1 Shir hama-alōs, b'shuv adōnoy
es shivas tziyōn hoyinu
k'chōlmim. Oz yimolay
s'chōk pinu ulshōnaynu rinoh,
oz yōm'ru vagōyim higdil
adōnoy la-asōs im ayleh.
Higdil adōnoy la-asōs imonu
hoyinu s'maychim. Shuvoh adōnoy
es sh'visaynu ka-afikim
banegev. Hazōr-im b'dim-oh
b'rinoh yiktzōru. Holōch yaylaych
uvochōh nōsay meshech hazora,
bō yovō v'rinoh nōsay
alumōsov.

שִׁיר הַמַּעֲלוֹת, בְּשׁוּב יְיָ
אֶת־שִׁיבַת צִיּוֹן הָיִינוּ
כְּחֹלְמִים. אָז יִמָּלֵא
שְׂחוֹק פִּינוּ וּלְשׁוֹנֵנוּ רִנָּה,
אָז יֹאמְרוּ בַגּוֹיִם הִגְדִּיל
יְיָ לַעֲשׂוֹת עִם־אֵלֶּה.
הִגְדִּיל יְיָ לַעֲשׂוֹת עִמָּנוּ
הָיִינוּ שְׂמֵחִים. שׁוּבָה יְיָ
אֶת־שְׁבִיתֵנוּ כַּאֲפִיקִים
בַּנֶּגֶב. הַזֹּרְעִים בְּדִמְעָה
בְּרִנָּה יִקְצֹרוּ. הָלוֹךְ יֵלֵךְ
וּבָכֹה נֹשֵׂא מֶשֶׁךְ הַזָּרַע,
בֹּא־יָבֹא בְרִנָּה נֹשֵׂא
אֲלֻמֹּתָיו.

T'hilas adōnoy y'daber pi, vivoraych
kol bosor shaym kodshō
l'ōlom vo-ed. Va-anachnu
n'voraych yoh may-atoh v'ad
ōlom hal'luyoh. Hōdu ladōnoy
ki tōv ki l'ōlom chasdō.
Mi y'malayl g'vurōs adōnoy
yashmi-a kol t'hilosō.

תְּהִלַּת יְיָ יְדַבֶּר פִּי, וִיבָרֵךְ
כָּל־בָּשָׂר שֵׁם קָדְשׁוֹ
לְעוֹלָם וָעֶד. וַאֲנַחְנוּ
נְבָרֵךְ יָהּ מֵעַתָּה וְעַד
עוֹלָם הַלְלוּיָהּ. הוֹדוּ לַיְיָ
כִּי־טוֹב כִּי לְעוֹלָם חַסְדּוֹ.
מִי יְמַלֵּל גְּבוּרוֹת יְיָ
יַשְׁמִיעַ כָּל־תְּהִלָּתוֹ.

A Song of Ascents. When the Lord brought Zion out of captivity, we were
like people in a dream. At that time our mouth was filled with laughter and
our tongue with cries of joy; at that time it was said among the nations, "The

Lord has done great things for them." The Lord had done great things for us; we were happy. Let our captivity, Lord, be a thing of the past, like dried-up streams in the Negev. Those who sow in tears shall reap in joy. The man who weeps as he trails the seed along will return with cries of joy, carrying his sheaves.

Now let my mouth declare the Lord's praise, and let the whole human race bless His holy name for all time. As for us, we will bless the Lord from now on and forever more: Praise the Lord! Give thanks to the Lord for He is good, for His kindness is everlasting! Who can describe the mighty deeds of the Lord, or utter all His praise?

When three or more men have eaten together, one invites the others to join him in the Blessing after the Meal:

2 *Rabōsai n'voraych.*　　　　　　　　　　　רַבּוֹתַי נְבָרֵךְ.

My friends, let us say the blessing.

The others answer

Y'hi shaym adōnoy m'vōroch may-atoh　　　יְהִי שֵׁם יְיָ מְבֹרָךְ מֵעַתָּה
v'ad ōlom.　　　　　　　　　　　　　　　וְעַד־עוֹלָם.

May the name of the Lord be blessed from now on and forever more.

The leader repeats

Y'hi shaym adōnoy m'vōroch may-atoh　　　יְהִי שֵׁם יְיָ מְבֹרָךְ מֵעַתָּה
v'ad ōlom.　　　　　　　　　　　　　　　וְעַד־עוֹלָם.

May the name of the Lord be blessed from now on and forever more.

and he continues

Birshus　　　　　　　　　　　　　　　　　בִּרְשׁוּת

If his father is present he adds

ovi mōri אָבִי מוֹרִי

If he is a guest at someone else's table he adds

ba-al habayis בַּעַל הַבַּיִת

60

moronon v'rabonon v'rabōsai n'voraych מָרָנָן וְרַבָּנָן וְרַבּוֹתַי נְבָרֵךְ

If there are ten men present he adds

elōhaynu אֱלֹהֵינוּ

she-ochalnu mishelō. שֶׁאָכַלְנוּ מִשֶּׁלּוֹ.

With the consent of (my honored father and) (our host and) all present, let us bless Him (our God) whose food we have eaten.

The others say

Boruch (elōhaynu) she-ochalnu בָּרוּךְ (אֱלֹהֵינוּ) שֶׁאָכַלְנוּ
mishelō uvtuvō choyinu. מִשֶּׁלּוֹ וּבְטוּבוֹ חָיִינוּ.

Blessed is He (our God) whose food we have eaten and through whose goodness we live.

The leader repeats

Boruch (elōhaynu) she-ochalnu בָּרוּךְ (אֱלֹהֵינוּ) שֶׁאָכַלְנוּ
mishelō uvtuvō choyinu. מִשֶּׁלּוֹ וּבְטוּבוֹ חָיִינוּ.

Blessed is He (our God) whose food we have eaten and through whose goodness we live.

All say

Boruch hu uvoruch sh'mō. בָּרוּךְ הוּא וּבָרוּךְ שְׁמוֹ.

May He be blessed and may His name be blessed.

Individuals begin here:

3 *Boruch atoh adōnoy, elōhaynu* בָּרוּךְ אַתָּה יְיָ, אֱלֹהֵינוּ
melech ho-ōlom, hazon es מֶלֶךְ הָעוֹלָם, הַזָּן אֶת־
ho-ōlom kulō b'tuvō b'chayn הָעוֹלָם כֻּלּוֹ בְּטוּבוֹ בְּחֵן
b'chesed uvrachamim hu בְּחֶסֶד וּבְרַחֲמִים הוּא
nōsayn lechem l'chol bosor, ki נוֹתֵן לֶחֶם לְכָל־בָּשָׂר, כִּי
l'ōlom chasdō. Uv'tuvō לְעוֹלָם חַסְדּוֹ. וּבְטוּבוֹ

61

hagodōl tomid lō chosar	הַגָּדוֹל תָּמִיד לֹא־חָסַר
lonu v'al yechsar lonu mozōn	לָנוּ וְאַל־יֶחְסַר לָנוּ מָזוֹן
l'ōlom vo-ed. Ba-avur sh'mō	לְעוֹלָם וָעֶד. בַּעֲבוּר שְׁמוֹ
hagodōl ki hu ayl zon	הַגָּדוֹל כִּי הוּא אֵל זָן
umfarnays lakōl umaytiv lakōl	וּמְפַרְנֵס לַכֹּל וּמֵטִיב לַכֹּל
umaychin mozōn l'chol b'riyōsov	וּמֵכִין מָזוֹן לְכָל־בְּרִיּוֹתָיו
asher boro. Boruch atoh	אֲשֶׁר בָּרָא. בָּרוּךְ אַתָּה
adōnoy, hazon es hakōl.	יְיָ, הַזָּן אֶת־הַכֹּל.

You are blessed, Lord our God, the sovereign of the world, who provides food for the entire world in His goodness, with grace, kindness and mercy; He supplies bread for all living beings, for His kindness is everlasting. Because of His great goodness, we have never lacked food, nor will we ever lack it—on account of His great name—since He is God who feeds and provides for all and is good to all, and who supplies food for all His creatures which He brought into being. You are blessed, Lord, who provides food for all.

4 Nōdeh l'cho adōnoy elōhaynu al	נוֹדֶה לְךָ יְיָ אֱלֹהֵינוּ עַל
shehinchalto la-avōsaynu eretz	שֶׁהִנְחַלְתָּ לַאֲבוֹתֵינוּ אֶרֶץ
chemdoh tōvoh urchovoh,	חֶמְדָּה טוֹבָה וּרְחָבָה,
v'al shehōtzaysonu adōnoy	וְעַל שֶׁהוֹצֵאתָנוּ יְיָ
elōhaynu may-eretz mitzra-yim	אֱלֹהֵינוּ מֵאֶרֶץ מִצְרַיִם
ufdisonu mibays avodim,	וּפְדִיתָנוּ מִבֵּית עֲבָדִים,
v'al b'ris'cho shechosamto	וְעַל בְּרִיתְךָ שֶׁחָתַמְתָּ
bivsoraynu, v'al tōros-cho	בִּבְשָׂרֵנוּ, וְעַל תּוֹרָתְךָ
shelimadtonu, v'al chukecho	שֶׁלִּמַּדְתָּנוּ, וְעַל חֻקֶּיךָ
shehōdo-tanu, v'al cha-yim chayn	שֶׁהוֹדַעְתָּנוּ, וְעַל חַיִּים חֵן
vochesed shechōnantonu, v'al	וָחֶסֶד שֶׁחוֹנַנְתָּנוּ, וְעַל
achilas mozōn sho-atoh zon	אֲכִילַת מָזוֹן שָׁאַתָּה זָן
umfarnays ōsonu tomid	וּמְפַרְנֵס אוֹתָנוּ תָּמִיד
b'chol yōm uvchol ays	בְּכָל־יוֹם וּבְכָל־עֵת
uvchol sho-oh.	וּבְכָל־שָׁעָה.

We thank You, Lord our God, for having given the heritage of a lovely, fine and spacious land to our fathers, and for having brought us out, Lord our God, from Egypt, and for rescuing us from slavery, and also for Your covenant which You sealed in our flesh, as well as for Your Torah which You taught us, and Your laws of which You told us, and for the life, grace and kindness You have granted us, and for the food which You supply and provide for us constantly, every day, all the time, and at every hour.

On Chanukkah

5 *Al hanisim v'al hapurkon*   עַל הַנִּסִּים וְעַל הַפֻּרְקָן

v'al hagvurōs v'al   וְעַל הַגְּבוּרוֹת וְעַל

hat-shu-ōs v'al   הַתְּשׁוּעוֹת וְעַל

hamilchomōs she-osiso   הַמִּלְחָמוֹת שֶׁעָשִׂיתָ

la-avōsaynu ba-yomim hohaym   לַאֲבוֹתֵינוּ בַּיָּמִים הָהֵם

bazman hazeh.   בַּזְּמַן הַזֶּה.

We thank You for the miracles, for the liberation, for the mighty acts, for the victories, and for the wars which You waged for our ancestors in those days on this occasion.

Bimay matisyohu ben yōchonon   בִּימֵי מַתִּתְיָהוּ בֶּן־יוֹחָנָן

kōhayn godōl chashmōnai uvonov.   כֹּהֵן גָּדוֹל חַשְׁמוֹנַי וּבָנָיו.

K'she-omdoh malchus yovon   כְּשֶׁעָמְדָה מַלְכוּת יָוָן

horsho-oh al amcho yisro-ayl   הָרְשָׁעָה עַל עַמְּךָ יִשְׂרָאֵל

l'hashkichom tōrosecho   לְהַשְׁכִּיחָם תּוֹרָתֶךָ

ulha-avirom maychukay r'tzōnecho.   וּלְהַעֲבִירָם מֵחֻקֵּי רְצוֹנֶךָ.

V'atoh b'rachamecho horabim   וְאַתָּה בְּרַחֲמֶיךָ הָרַבִּים

omadto lohem b'ays tzorosom   עָמַדְתָּ לָהֶם בְּעֵת צָרָתָם

ravto es rivom danto es   רַבְתָּ אֶת־רִיבָם דַּנְתָּ אֶת־

dinom nokamto es nikmosom   דִּינָם נָקַמְתָּ אֶת־נִקְמָתָם

mosarto gibōrim   מָסַרְתָּ גִבּוֹרִים

b'yad chaloshim v'rabim b'yad   בְּיַד חַלָּשִׁים וְרַבִּים בְּיַד

m'atim utmay-im b'yad   מְעַטִּים וּטְמֵאִים בְּיַד

t'hōrim ursho-im b'yad   טְהוֹרִים וּרְשָׁעִים בְּיַד

tzadikim v'zaydim b'yad ōskay	צַדִּיקִים וְזֵדִים בְּיַד עוֹסְקֵי
sōrosecho. Ul'cho osiso shaym	תוֹרָתֶךָ. וּלְךָ עָשִׂיתָ שֵׁם
godōl v'kodōsh b'ōlomecho	גָּדוֹל וְקָדוֹשׁ בְּעוֹלָמֶךָ
ul-amcho yisro-ayl osiso	וּלְעַמְּךָ יִשְׂרָאֵל עָשִׂיתָ
t'shu-oh g'dōloh ufurkon	תְּשׁוּעָה גְדוֹלָה וּפֻרְקָן
k'ha-yōm hazeh. V'achar kayn	כְּהַיּוֹם הַזֶּה. וְאַחַר כֵּן
bov vonecho lidvir baysecho	בָּאוּ בָנֶיךָ לִדְבִיר בֵּיתֶךָ
ufinu es haycholecho v'tiharu	וּפִנּוּ אֶת־הֵיכָלֶךָ וְטִהֲרוּ
es mikdoshecho v'hidliku	אֶת־מִקְדָּשֶׁךָ וְהִדְלִיקוּ
nayrōs b'chatzrōs kodshecho	נֵרוֹת בְּחַצְרוֹת קָדְשֶׁךָ
v'kovu sh'mōnas y'may chanukoh	וְקָבְעוּ שְׁמוֹנַת יְמֵי חֲנֻכָּה
aylu l'hōdōs ulhalayl	אֵלּוּ לְהוֹדוֹת וּלְהַלֵּל
l'shimcho hagodōl.	לְשִׁמְךָ הַגָּדוֹל.

It was in the days of Mattathias, son of Yohanan, the High Priest, a Hasmonean, and his sons, that the wicked Hellenistic regime confronted Your people Israel to make them forget Your Torah and to drive them away from the laws of Your will. Then You, in Your great mercy, stood up for them in their time of trouble. You pleaded their cause, argued their case, and avenged their wrong; You delivered the strong into the power of the weak, the many into the power of the few, the impure into the power of the pure, the wicked into the power of the righteous, and the sacreligious into the power of those immersed in Your Torah. Thus You made for Yourself a great and holy name in Your world, and for Your people Israel You brought about a great victory and liberation on this day. And afterwards, Your children came to the sanctuary of Your house, cleared Your holy place, purified Your temple, and kindled lights in Your holy courts, and they established these eight days of Chanukkah for giving thanks and praise to Your great name.

On Purim

6 Al hanisim v'al hapurkon	עַל הַנִּסִּים וְעַל הַפֻּרְקָן
v'al hagvurōs v'al	וְעַל הַגְּבוּרוֹת וְעַל
hat-shu-ōs v'al	הַתְּשׁוּעוֹת וְעַל

hamilchomōs she-osiso	הַמִּלְחָמוֹת שֶׁעָשִׂיתָ
la-avōsaynu ba-yomim hohaym	לַאֲבוֹתֵינוּ בַּיָּמִים הָהֵם
bazman hazeh.	בַּזְּמַן הַזֶּה.

We thank You for the miracles, for the liberation, for the mighty acts, for the victories, and for the wars which You waged for our ancestors in those days on this occasion.

Bimay mord'chai v'estayr	בִּימֵי מָרְדְּכַי וְאֶסְתֵּר
b'shushan habiroh k'she-omad	בְּשׁוּשַׁן הַבִּירָה כְּשֶׁעָמַד
alayhem homon horosho.	עֲלֵיהֶם הָמָן הָרָשָׁע.
Bikaysh l'hashmid laharōg	בִּקֵּשׁ לְהַשְׁמִיד לַהֲרֹג
ul-abayd es kol ha-y'hudim	וּלְאַבֵּד אֶת־כָּל־הַיְּהוּדִים
mina-ar v'ad zokayn taf v'noshim	מִנַּעַר וְעַד־זָקֵן טַף וְנָשִׁים
b'yōm echod bishlōshoh osor	בְּיוֹם אֶחָד בִּשְׁלֹשָׁה עָשָׂר
l'chōdesh sh'naym osor hu	לְחֹדֶשׁ שְׁנֵים־עָשָׂר הוּא
chōdesh ador ushlolom lovōz.	חֹדֶשׁ אֲדָר וּשְׁלָלָם לָבוֹז.
V'atoh b'rachamecho horabim	וְאַתָּה בְּרַחֲמֶיךָ הָרַבִּים
hayfarto es atzosō	הֵפַרְתָּ אֶת־עֲצָתוֹ
v'kilkalto es machashavtō	וְקִלְקַלְתָּ אֶת־מַחֲשַׁבְתּוֹ
vahashayvōso g'mulō b'rōshō	וַהֲשֵׁבוֹתָ גְּמוּלוֹ בְּרֹאשׁוֹ
v'solu ōsō v'es bonov	וְתָלוּ אוֹתוֹ וְאֶת־בָּנָיו
al ho-aytz.	עַל־הָעֵץ.

It was in the days of Mordecai and Esther, in the capital city of Shushan, that the wicked Haman rose up against them, seeking to wipe out, to murder and to destroy all the Jews, young and old, women and children, on one day, on the thirteenth day of the twelfth month, which is the month of Adar, plundering them for spoil. But you, in Your great mercy, frustrated his plan, and thwarted his intention, and turned the tables on him, so that they hung him and his sons on the gallows.

7   *V'al hakōl adōnoy elōhaynu*   וְעַל הַכֹּל יְיָ אֱלֹהֵינוּ

anachnu mōdim loch   אֲנַחְנוּ מוֹדִים לָךְ

umvorchim ōsoch yisborach   וּמְבָרְכִים אוֹתָךְ יִתְבָּרַךְ

shimcho b'fi chol chai tomid   שִׁמְךָ בְּפִי כָל־חַי תָּמִיד

l'ōlom vo-ed. Kakosuv,   לְעוֹלָם וָעֶד. כַּכָּתוּב,

v'ochalto v'sovo-to uvayrachto   וְאָכַלְתָּ וְשָׂבָעְתָּ וּבֵרַכְתָּ

es adōnoy elōhecho al ho-oretz   אֶת־יְיָ אֱלֹהֶיךָ עַל־הָאָרֶץ

hatōvoh asher nosan loch.   הַטֹּבָה אֲשֶׁר נָתַן־לָךְ.

Boruch atoh adōnoy, al ho-oretz   בָּרוּךְ אַתָּה יְיָ, עַל־הָאָרֶץ

v'al hamozōn.   וְעַל־הַמָּזוֹן.

So for everything, Lord our God, we thank You and bless You—may Your name be blessed in the speech of all living beings, constantly, for all time. For it is written: "And you shall eat, and be satisfied, and bless the Lord Your God for the good land He gave you." You are blessed, Lord, for the land and for the food.

8   *Rachaym adōnoy elōhaynu al*   רַחֵם יְיָ אֱלֹהֵינוּ עַל־

yisro-ayl amecho v'al   יִשְׂרָאֵל עַמֶּךָ וְעַל

y'rushola-yim irecho v'al tziyōn   יְרוּשָׁלַיִם עִירֶךָ וְעַל צִיּוֹן

mishkan k'vōdecho v'al   מִשְׁכַּן כְּבוֹדֶךָ וְעַל

malchus bays dovid m'shichecho   מַלְכוּת בֵּית דָּוִד מְשִׁיחֶךָ

v'al haba-yis hagodōl   וְעַל הַבַּיִת הַגָּדוֹל

v'hakodōsh shenikro shimcho   וְהַקָּדוֹשׁ שֶׁנִּקְרָא שִׁמְךָ

olov. Elōhaynu ovinu r'aynu   עָלָיו. אֱלֹהֵינוּ אָבִינוּ רְעֵנוּ

zunaynu parn'saynu v'chalk'laynu   זוּנֵנוּ פַּרְנְסֵנוּ וְכַלְכְּלֵנוּ

v'harvichaynu v'harvach lonu adōnoy   וְהַרְוִיחֵנוּ וְהַרְוַח־לָנוּ יְיָ

elōhaynu m'hayroh mikol   אֱלֹהֵינוּ מְהֵרָה מִכָּל־

tzorōsaynu. V'no al   צָרוֹתֵינוּ. וְנָא אַל־

tatzrichaynu adōnoy elōhaynu lō   תַּצְרִיכֵנוּ יְיָ אֱלֹהֵינוּ לֹא

liday matnas bosor vodom   לִידֵי מַתְּנַת בָּשָׂר וָדָם

v'lō liday halvo-osom, ki	וְלֹא לִידֵי הַלְוָאָתָם, כִּי
im l'yodcho hamlay-oh	אִם לְיָדְךָ הַמְּלֵאָה
hapsuchoh hakdōshoh	הַפְּתוּחָה הַקְּדוֹשָׁה
v'horchovoh, shelō nayvōsh	וְהָרְחָבָה, שֶׁלֹּא נֵבוֹשׁ
v'lō nikolaym l'ōlom vo-ed.	וְלֹא נִכָּלֵם לְעוֹלָם וָעֶד.

Have mercy, Lord our God, on Israel Your people, on Jerusalem, Your city, on Zion the home of Your glory, on the kingdom of the house of David Your anointed one, and on the great and holy house which is called by Your name. Our God, our Father—look after us and feed us, give us a livelihood and support us, and provide a respite for us—a respite for us, Lord our God, soon, from all our troubles. And please, let us not be dependent, Lord our God, neither on a gift, nor on a loan from a human being, but rather on Your full, open, holy and generous hand, so that we should never feel embarrassed or ashamed.

On Shabbos

9 R'tzayh v'hachalitzaynu adōnoy	רְצֵה וְהַחֲלִיצֵנוּ יְיָ
elōhaynu b'mitzvōsecho	אֱלֹהֵינוּ בְּמִצְוֹתֶיךָ
uvmitzvas yōm hashvi-i	וּבְמִצְוַת יוֹם הַשְּׁבִיעִי
hashabbos hagodōl v'hakodōsh	הַשַּׁבָּת הַגָּדוֹל וְהַקָּדוֹשׁ
hazeh. Ki yōm zeh godōl	הַזֶּה. כִּי יוֹם זֶה גָּדוֹל
v'kodōsh hu l'fonecho	וְקָדוֹשׁ הוּא לְפָנֶיךָ
lishbos bō v'lonuach bō	לִשְׁבָּת־בּוֹ וְלָנוּחַ בּוֹ
b'ahavoh k'mitzvas r'tzōnecho.	בְּאַהֲבָה כְּמִצְוַת רְצוֹנֶךָ.
Uvirtzōncho honiyach lonu adōnoy	וּבִרְצוֹנְךָ הָנִיחַ לָנוּ יְיָ
elōhaynu shelō s'hay tzoroh	אֱלֹהֵינוּ שֶׁלֹּא תְהֵא צָרָה
v'yogōn va-anochoh b'yōm	וְיָגוֹן וַאֲנָחָה בְּיוֹם
m'nuchosaynu. V'har-aynu adōnoy	מְנוּחָתֵנוּ. וְהַרְאֵנוּ יְיָ
elōhaynu b'nechomas tziyōn	אֱלֹהֵינוּ בְּנֶחָמַת צִיּוֹן
irecho uv'vinyan y'rushola-yim	עִירֶךָ וּבְבִנְיַן יְרוּשָׁלַיִם
ir kodshecho ki atoh hu	עִיר קָדְשֶׁךָ כִּי אַתָּה הוּא

ba-al ha-y'shu-ōs uva-al
hanechomōs.

בַּעַל הַיְשׁוּעוֹת וּבַעַל
הַנֶּחָמוֹת.

Be pleased, Lord our God, to strengthen us through Your commandments, especially the commandment of the seventh day, this great and holy Shabbos. For this is indeed a great and holy day for You; to rest and to be at ease, with loving concern for the command of Your will. So may it please You to grant us rest, Lord our God, with no trouble, or unhappiness, or weeping on our day of rest. And let us witness, Lord our God, the consolation of Zion, Your city, and the building up of Jerusalem, Your holy city, for You are the Lord of redemption, and the Lord of consolation.

On Rosh Chodesh and Yom Tov

10 Elōhaynu vaylōhay avōsaynu,
ya-aleh v'yovō v'yagi-a v'yayro-eh
v'yayrotzeh v'yishoma v'yipokayd
v'yizochayr zichrōnaynu ufikdōnaynu,
v'zichrōn avōsaynu, v'zichrōn
moshiyach ben dovid avdecho,
v'zichrōn y'rushola-yim ir
kodshecho, v'zichrōn kol amcho
bays yisro-ayl l'fonecho,
liflaytoh ultōvoh ulchayn
ulchesed ulrachamim ulcha-yim
ulsholōm b'yōm

אֱלֹהֵינוּ וֵאלֹהֵי אֲבוֹתֵינוּ,
יַעֲלֶה וְיָבֹא וְיַגִּיעַ וְיֵרָאֶה
וְיֵרָצֶה וְיִשָּׁמַע וְיִפָּקֵד
וְיִזָּכֵר זִכְרוֹנֵנוּ וּפִקְדוֹנֵנוּ,
וְזִכְרוֹן אֲבוֹתֵינוּ, וְזִכְרוֹן
מָשִׁיחַ בֶּן־דָּוִד עַבְדֶּךָ,
וְזִכְרוֹן יְרוּשָׁלַיִם עִיר
קָדְשֶׁךָ, וְזִכְרוֹן כָּל־עַמְּךָ
בֵּית יִשְׂרָאֵל לְפָנֶיךָ,
לִפְלֵיטָה וּלְטוֹבָה וּלְחֵן
וּלְחֶסֶד וּלְרַחֲמִים וּלְחַיִּים
וּלְשָׁלוֹם בְּיוֹם

Rosh Chodesh

rōsh hachōdesh hazeh.

רֹאשׁ הַחֹדֶשׁ הַזֶּה.

Rosh Hashanah

hazikorōn hazeh.

הַזִּכָּרוֹן הַזֶּה.

Sukkos

chag hasukōs hazeh.

חַג הַסֻּכּוֹת הַזֶּה.

68

Sh'mini Atzeres and Simchas Torah

hashmini chag ho-atzeres
hazeh.

הַשְּׁמִינִי חַג הָעֲצֶרֶת
הַזֶּה.

Pesach

chag hamatzōs hazeh.

חַג הַמַּצּוֹת הַזֶּה.

Shavuos

chag hashovu-ōs hazeh.

חַג הַשָּׁבֻעוֹת הַזֶּה.

Zochraynu adōnoy elōhaynu bō
l'tōvoh ufokdaynu vō
livrochoh v'hōshi-aynu vō
l'cha-yim. Uvidvar y'shu-oh
v'rachamim chus v'chonaynu v'rachaym
olaynu v'hōshi-aynu, ki
aylecho aynaynu, ki ayl melech
chanun v'rachum otoh.

זָכְרֵנוּ יְיָ אֱלֹהֵינוּ בּוֹ
לְטוֹבָה וּפָקְדֵנוּ בוֹ
לִבְרָכָה וְהוֹשִׁיעֵנוּ בוֹ
לְחַיִּים. וּבִדְבַר יְשׁוּעָה
וְרַחֲמִים חוּס וְחָנֵּנוּ וְרַחֵם
עָלֵינוּ וְהוֹשִׁיעֵנוּ, כִּי
אֵלֶיךָ עֵינֵינוּ, כִּי אֵל מֶלֶךְ
חַנּוּן וְרַחוּם אָתָּה.

Our God and God of our fathers, may a reminder and a remembrance of us, and of our fathers, and of the Messiah the son of David Your servant, and of Jerusalem Your holy city, and of all Your people the house of Israel, ascend and arrive, reach and be noticed, and accepted, heard, noted and remembered before You, for deliverance and well-being, for grace, kindness and mercy, for life and peace—on this day of

the New Month/Remembrance/the Festival of Sukkos/the Eighth Day of Assembly Festival/the Festival of Unleavened Bread/the Festival of Shavuos.

Be mindful of us, Lord our God, on this day, for good, take note of us for blessing and preserve us in life. And with an act of redemption and mercy, have pity on us and be gracious to us, and be merciful to us and save us, for our eyes are directed toward You, for You are a gracious and merciful divine ruler.

11 *Uvnayh y'rushola-yim ir*   וּבְנֵה יְרוּשָׁלַיִם עִיר
hakōdesh bimhayroh v'yomaynu.   הַקֹדֶשׁ בִּמְהֵרָה בְיָמֵינוּ.
Boruch atoh adōnoy, bōneh   בָּרוּךְ אַתָּה יְיָ, בּוֹנֵה
v'rachamov y'rusholoyim. Omayn.   בְּרַחֲמָיו יְרוּשָׁלָיִם. אָמֵן.

And may You build up Jerusalem, the holy city, rapidly in our lifetimes,
You are blessed, Lord, who in His mercy, builds up Jerusalem. Amen.

12 *Boruch atoh adōnoy, elōhaynu*   בָּרוּךְ אַתָּה יְיָ, אֱלֹהֵינוּ
melech ho-ōlom, ho-ayl ovinu   מֶלֶךְ הָעוֹלָם, הָאֵל אָבִינוּ
malkaynu adiraynu bōr-aynu   מַלְכֵּנוּ אַדִּירֵנוּ בּוֹרְאֵנוּ
gō-alaynu yōtzraynu k'dōshaynu   גֹּאֲלֵנוּ יוֹצְרֵנוּ קְדוֹשֵׁנוּ
k'dōsh ya-akōv, rō-aynu rō-ayh   קְדוֹשׁ יַעֲקֹב, רוֹעֵנוּ רוֹעֵה
yisro-ayl hamelech hatōv   יִשְׂרָאֵל הַמֶּלֶךְ הַטּוֹב
v'hamaytiv lakōl shebchol yōm   וְהַמֵּטִיב לַכֹּל שֶׁבְּכָל־יוֹם
voyōm hu haytiv hu   וָיוֹם הוּא הֵטִיב הוּא
maytiv hu yaytiv lonu.   מֵטִיב הוּא יֵטִיב לָנוּ.
Hu g'molonu hu gōmlaynu   הוּא גְמָלָנוּ הוּא גוֹמְלֵנוּ
hu yigm'laynu lo-ad l'chayn   הוּא יִגְמְלֵנוּ לָעַד לְחֵן
l'chesed ulrachamim ulrevach   לְחֶסֶד וּלְרַחֲמִים וּלְרֶוַח
hatzoloh v'hatzlochoh b'rochoh   הַצָּלָה וְהַצְלָחָה בְּרָכָה
vishu-oh nechomoh parnosoh   וִישׁוּעָה נֶחָמָה פַּרְנָסָה
v'chalkoloh v'rachamim v'cha-yim   וְכַלְכָּלָה וְרַחֲמִים וְחַיִּים
v'sholōm v'chol tōv, umikol   וְשָׁלוֹם וְכָל־טוֹב, וּמִכָּל־
tōv l'ōlom al y'chasraynu.   טוֹב לְעוֹלָם אַל־יְחַסְּרֵנוּ.

You are blessed, Lord our God, the sovereign of the world—God who is
our father, our king, our mighty one, our creator, our redeemer, our maker,
our holy one—the holy one of Jacob; our shepherd—the shepherd of Israel;
the king who is good and who does good to all, who each and every day has
been good, is good and will be good to us. He gave, gives, and will always give
us grace, kindness and mercy, and respite, deliverance and success, blessing

and salvation, comfort, a livelihood and sustenance, and mercy and life and peace and everything that is good—and may He never let us lack anything that is good.

13 *Horachamon hu yimlōch olaynu l'ōlom vo-ed. Horachamon hu yisborach bashoma-yim uvo-oretz.*
Horachamon hu yishtabach l'dōr dōrim v'yispo-ar bonu l'naytzach n'tzochim v'yis-hadar bonu lo-ad ul-ōlmay ōlomim. Horachamon hu y'farn'saynu b'chovōd. Horachamon hu yishbōr ulaynu may-al tzavoraynu v'hu yōlichaynu kōmami-us l'artzaynu.
Horachamon hu yishlach b'rochoh m'ruboh baba-yis hazeh v'al shulchon zeh she-ochalnu olov. Horachamon hu yishlach lonu es ayliyohu hanovi zochur latōv vivaser lonu b'sōrōs tōvōs y'shu-ōs v'nechomōs.

הָרַחֲמָן הוּא יִמְלֹךְ עָלֵינוּ
לְעוֹלָם וָעֶד. הָרַחֲמָן הוּא
יִתְבָּרֵךְ בַּשָּׁמַיִם וּבָאָרֶץ.
הָרַחֲמָן הוּא יִשְׁתַּבַּח
לְדוֹר דּוֹרִים וְיִתְפָּאַר בָּנוּ
לָנֶצַח נְצָחִים וְיִתְהַדַּר
בָּנוּ לָעַד וּלְעוֹלְמֵי
עוֹלָמִים. הָרַחֲמָן הוּא
יְפַרְנְסֵנוּ בְּכָבוֹד. הָרַחֲמָן
הוּא יִשְׁבֹּר עֻלֵּנוּ מֵעַל
צַוָּארֵנוּ וְהוּא יוֹלִיכֵנוּ
קוֹמְמִיּוּת לְאַרְצֵנוּ.
הָרַחֲמָן הוּא יִשְׁלַח
בְּרָכָה מְרֻבָּה בַּבַּיִת הַזֶּה
וְעַל שֻׁלְחָן זֶה שֶׁאָכַלְנוּ
עָלָיו. הָרַחֲמָן הוּא יִשְׁלַח
לָנוּ אֶת־אֵלִיָּהוּ הַנָּבִיא
זָכוּר לַטּוֹב וִיבַשֶּׂר־לָנוּ
בְּשׂוֹרוֹת טוֹבוֹת יְשׁוּעוֹת
וְנֶחָמוֹת.

The Merciful One—He will rule over us forever. May the Merciful One be blessed in heaven and on earth. May the Merciful One be praised for generation upon generation, and may He be glorified through us forever and ever, and may He be honored through us eternally. May the Merciful One grant us an honorable livelihood. May the Merciful One break the yoke from our neck and lead us upright to our land. May the Merciful One send a plentiful blessing on this house and on this table at which we have eaten. May the Merciful One send us Elijah the prophet—who is remembered for good— who will bring us good tidings of salvation and comfort.

14 *Horachamon hu y'voraych*   הָרַחֲמָן הוּא יְבָרֵךְ

May the Merciful One bless

for one's parents

es ovi mōri (ba-al	אֶת־אָבִי מוֹרִי (בַּעַל
haba-yis hazeh) v'es imi	הַבַּיִת הַזֶּה) וְאֶת־אִמִּי
mōrosi (ba-alas haba-yis	מוֹרָתִי (בַּעֲלַת הַבַּיִת
hazeh), ōsom v'es baysom	הַזֶּה), אוֹתָם וְאֶת־בֵּיתָם
v'es zar-om v'es kol	וְאֶת־זַרְעָם וְאֶת־כָּל־
asher lohem,	אֲשֶׁר לָהֶם,

my honored father (the man of this house) and my honored mother (the woman of this house) them, together with their household, their children and everything that is theirs.

for oneself and one's own family

ōsi v'es ishti (ba-ali)	אוֹתִי וְאֶת־אִשְׁתִּי (בַּעֲלִי)
v'es zar-i v'es kol asher	וְאֶת־זַרְעִי וְאֶת־כָּל־אֲשֶׁר
li,	לִי,

me, my wife (my husband), together with everything that is mine,

for one's hosts

es ba-al haba-yis hazeh	אֶת־בַּעַל הַבַּיִת הַזֶּה
v'es ba-alas haba-yis hazeh,	וְאֶת־בַּעֲלַת הַבַּיִת הַזֶּה,
ōsom v'es baysom v'es	אוֹתָם וְאֶת־בֵּיתָם וְאֶת־
zar-om v'es kol asher	זַרְעָם וְאֶת־כָּל־אֲשֶׁר
lohem,	לָהֶם,

the man of this house and the woman of this house—them, together with their household, their children and everything that is theirs, v'es kol hamsubin kon,   וְאֶת־כָּל־הַמְסֻבִּין כָּאן,

and all those who are seated here,

—ōsonu v'es kol asher   — אוֹתָנוּ וְאֶת־כָּל־אֲשֶׁר

lonu, k'mō shenisborchu   לָנוּ, כְּמוֹ שֶׁנִּתְבָּרְכוּ

avōsaynu avrohom yitzchok   אֲבוֹתֵינוּ אַבְרָהָם יִצְחָק

v'ya-akōv bakōl mikōl kōl, kayn   וְיַעֲקֹב בַּכֹּל מִכֹּל כֹּל, כֵּן

y'voraych ōsonu kulonu yachad   יְבָרֵךְ אוֹתָנוּ כֻּלָּנוּ יַחַד

bivrochoh sh'laymoh, v'nōmar   בִּבְרָכָה שְׁלֵמָה, וְנֹאמַר

omayn.   אָמֵן.

—us, together with all that is ours, just as our fathers, Abraham, Isaac and Jacob, were blessed—totally—so may He bless us, all of us together, with a complete blessing, and let us say, Amen.

15 Bamorōm y'lamdu alayhem   בַּמָּרוֹם יְלַמְּדוּ עֲלֵיהֶם

v'olaynu z'chus shet-hay   וְעָלֵינוּ זְכוּת שֶׁתְּהֵא

l'mishmeres sholōm. V'niso   לְמִשְׁמֶרֶת שָׁלוֹם. וְנִשָּׂא

v'rochoh may-ays adōnoy utzdokoh   בְרָכָה מֵאֵת יְיָ וּצְדָקָה

may-elōhay yish-aynu. V'nimtzo   מֵאֱלֹהֵי יִשְׁעֵנוּ. וְנִמְצָא־

chayn v'saychel tōv b'aynay   חֵן וְשֵׂכֶל טוֹב בְּעֵינֵי

elōhim v'odom.   אֱלֹהִים וְאָדָם.

May a plea be heard on high, for them and for us, which will result in the security of peace. So may we receive a blessing from the Lord and righteousness from the God of our salvation. So may we find favor and understanding in the sight of God and man.

On Shabbos

16 Horachamon hu yanchilaynu yōm   הָרַחֲמָן הוּא יַנְחִילֵנוּ יוֹם

shekulō shabbos umnuchoh   שֶׁכֻּלּוֹ שַׁבָּת וּמְנוּחָה

l'cha-yay ho-ōlomim.   לְחַיֵּי הָעוֹלָמִים.

May the Merciful One bring us the day which will be totally Shabbos and rest, in everlasting life.

On Rosh Chodesh

Horachamon hu y'chadaysh olaynu הָרַחֲמָן הוּא יְחַדֵּשׁ עָלֵינוּ
es hachōdesh hazeh l'tōvoh אֶת־הַחֹדֶשׁ הַזֶּה לְטוֹבָה
v'livrochoh. וְלִבְרָכָה.

May the Merciful One introduce this month to us with goodness and blessing.

On Yom Tov

Horachamon hu yanchilaynu yōm הָרַחֲמָן הוּא יַנְחִילֵנוּ יוֹם
shekulō tōv. שֶׁכֻּלוֹ טוֹב.

May the Merciful One bring us the day which will be totally good.

On Rosh Hashanah

Horachamon hu y'chadaysh olaynu הָרַחֲמָן הוּא יְחַדֵּשׁ עָלֵינוּ
es hashonoh hazōs l'tōvoh אֶת־הַשָּׁנָה הַזֹּאת לְטוֹבָה
v'livrochoh. וְלִבְרָכָה.

May the Merciful One introduce this year to us with goodness and blessing.

On Sukkos

Horachamon hu yokim lonu הָרַחֲמָן הוּא יָקִים לָנוּ
es sukas dovid hanōfeles. אֶת־סֻכַּת דָּוִד הַנֹּפָלֶת.

May the Merciful One raise up for us the fallen sukkah of David.

On other days, continue here

17 *Horachamon hu y'zakaynu limōs* הָרַחֲמָן הוּא יְזַכֵּנוּ לִימוֹת
hamoshiyach ulcha-yay ho-ōlom הַמָּשִׁיחַ וּלְחַיֵּי הָעוֹלָם
habo. הַבָּא.

May the Merciful One make us worthy of experiencing the days of the Messiah and the life of the world to come.

Migdōl	מַגְדּוֹל

Magdil	מַגְדִּיל

y'shu-ōs malkō v'ōseh	יְשׁוּעוֹת מַלְכּוֹ וְעֹשֶׂה
chesed limshichō l'dovid	חֶסֶד לִמְשִׁיחוֹ לְדָוִד
ulzar-ō ad ōlom. Ōseh	וּלְזַרְעוֹ עַד־עוֹלָם. עֹשֶׂה
sholōm bimrōmov hu	שָׁלוֹם בִּמְרוֹמָיו הוּא
ya-aseh sholōm olaynu v'al	יַעֲשֶׂה שָׁלוֹם עָלֵינוּ וְעַל
kol yisro-ayl, v'imru omayn.	כָּל־יִשְׂרָאֵל, וְאִמְרוּ אָמֵן.

He brings about great victories for His king and shows kindness to His anointed one—to David and to his descendants forever. He who makes peace in His high places, may He bring about peace for us and for all Israel, and say, Amen.

18	*Y'ru es adōnoy k'dōshov ki*	יְראוּ אֶת־יְיָ קְדֹשָׁיו כִּי
	ayn machsōr liray-ov.	אֵין מַחְסוֹר לִירֵאָיו.
	K'firim roshu v'ro-ayvu	כְּפִירִים רָשׁוּ וְרָעֵבוּ
	v'dōrshay adōnoy lō yachs'ru chol	וְדֹרְשֵׁי יְיָ לֹא־יַחְסְרוּ כָל־
	tōv. Hōdu ladōnoy ki tōv ki	טוֹב. הוֹדוּ לַייָ כִּי־טוֹב כִּי
	l'ōlom chasdō. Pōsayach	לְעוֹלָם חַסְדּוֹ. פּוֹתֵחַ
	es yodecho umasbi-a l'chol	אֶת־יָדֶךָ וּמַשְׂבִּיעַ לְכָל־
	chai rotzōn. Boruch hagever	חַי רָצוֹן. בָּרוּךְ הַגֶּבֶר
	asher yivtach badōnoy v'hoyoh adōnoy	אֲשֶׁר יִבְטַח בַּייָ וְהָיָה יְיָ
	mivtachō. Na-ar hoyisi	מִבְטַחוֹ. נַעַר הָיִיתִי
	gam zokanti v'lō ro-isi	גַּם־זָקַנְתִּי וְלֹא־רָאִיתִי
	tzadik ne-ezov v'zar-ō	צַדִּיק נֶעֱזָב וְזַרְעוֹ
	m'vakesh lochem. Adonoy ōz l'amō	מְבַקֶּשׁ־לָחֶם. יְיָ עֹז לְעַמּוֹ
	yitayn adōnoy y'voraych es amō	יִתֵּן יְיָ יְבָרֵךְ אֶת־עַמּוֹ
	vasholōm.	בַשָּׁלוֹם.

Stand in awe of the Lord, you who are His holy ones, for there is nothing lacking to those who stand in awe of Him. Even young lions suffer want and hunger, but those who seek the Lord will not lack any good thing. Give thanks to the Lord, for He is good, for His kindness is everlasting. You open Your hand and satisfy the desire of all living. Blessed is the man who trusts in the Lord, and who makes the Lord the object of his trust. I was young and I have become old, and yet I never overlooked a deserving man who was destitute, with his children begging for bread. May the Lord give strength to His people; May the Lord bless His people with peace.

When the Blessing after the Meal is said over wine:

Boruch atoh adōnoy,

elōhaynu melech ho-ōlom,

bōray p'ri hagofen.

בָּרוּךְ אַתָּה יְיָ,

אֱלֹהֵינוּ מֶלֶךְ הָעוֹלָם,

בּוֹרֵא פְּרִי הַגָּפֶן.

You are blessed, Lord our God, the sovereign of the world creator of the fruit of the vine.

בְּרָכָה מֵעֵין שָׁלֹשׁ ("עַל הַמִּחְיָה")
THE BLESSING AFTER A SNACK

This blessing is said after drinking wine or after eating one of the fruits (olives, dates, grapes, figs or pomegranates) or a product, other than bread, of one of the grains (wheat, barley, spelt, oats or rye) associated with the land of Israel

Boruch atoh adonoy,

elōhaynu melech ho-ōlom,

בָּרוּךְ אַתָּה יְיָ,

אֱלֹהֵינוּ מֶלֶךְ הָעוֹלָם,

You are blessed, Lord our God, the sovereign of the world,

for grain products

al hamichyoh v'al

hakalkoloh,

עַל הַמִּחְיָה וְעַל

הַכַּלְכָּלָה,

for the sustenance and nourishment

for fruits

al ho-aytz v'al p'ri ho-aytz,

עַל הָעֵץ וְעַל פְּרִי הָעֵץ,

for the trees and their fruit,

for wine

al hagefen v'al p'ri hagefen,

עַל הַגֶּפֶן וְעַל פְּרִי הַגֶּפֶן,

for the vine and its fruit,

for grain products and wine consumed together

al hamichyoh v'al

hakalkoloh v'al hagefen

v'al p'ri hagefen,

עַל הַמִּחְיָה וְעַל

הַכַּלְכָּלָה וְעַל הַגֶּפֶן

וְעַל פְּרִי הַגֶּפֶן,

for the sustenance and nourishment and the vine and its fruit

v'al t'nuvas hasodeh, v'al

`eretz chemdoh tōvoh

urchovoh sherotziso v'hinchalto

la-avōsaynu le-echōl mipiryoh

וְעַל תְּנוּבַת הַשָּׂדֶה, וְעַל

אֶרֶץ חֶמְדָּה טוֹבָה

וּרְחָבָה שֶׁרָצִיתָ וְהִנְחַלְתָּ

לַאֲבוֹתֵינוּ לֶאֱכֹל מִפִּרְיָהּ

v'lisbō-a mituvoh. Rachem	וְלִשְׂבֹּעַ מִטּוּבָהּ. רַחֶם־
no, adōnoy elōhaynu, al	נָא, יְיָ אֱלֹהֵינוּ, עַל
yisro-ayl amecho, v'al	יִשְׂרָאֵל עַמֶּךָ, וְעַל
y'rushola-yim irecho, v'al tziyōn	יְרוּשָׁלַיִם עִירֶךָ, וְעַל צִיּוֹן
mishkan k'vōdecho, v'al	מִשְׁכַּן כְּבוֹדֶךָ, וְעַל
mizbachacho v'al haycholecho.	מִזְבַּחֲךָ וְעַל הֵיכָלֶךָ.
Uv'nayh y'rushola-yim ir	וּבְנֵה יְרוּשָׁלַיִם עִיר
hakōdesh bimhayroh v'yomaynu,	הַקֹּדֶשׁ בִּמְהֵרָה בְיָמֵינוּ,
v'ha-alaynu l'sōchoh v'samchaynu	וְהַעֲלֵנוּ לְתוֹכָהּ וְשַׂמְּחֵנוּ
b'vinyonoh, v'nōchal mipiryoh	בְּבִנְיָנָהּ, וְנֹאכַל מִפִּרְיָהּ
v'nisba mituvoh, unvorech'cho	וְנִשְׂבַּע מִטּוּבָהּ, וּנְבָרֶכְךָ
oleho bikdushoh uvtohoroh,	עָלֶיהָ בִּקְדֻשָּׁה וּבְטָהֳרָה,

and for the produce, and for the lovely, fine and spacious land which You graciously gave to our ancestors as a heritage, to eat its fruit and to be sated with its goodness. Have mercy, Lord our God, on Israel Your people, on Jerusalem, Your city, on Zion the home of Your glory, on Your altar and on Your sanctuary. May You build up Jerusalem, the holy city, rapidly in our lifetimes. Bring us there so that we may rejoice in its rebuilding, eat of its fruit and be sated with its goodness. And there we will bless You in holiness and in purity,

on Shabbos

urtzayh v'hachalitzaynu b'yōm	וּרְצֵה וְהַחֲלִיצֵנוּ בְּיוֹם
hashabbos hazeh,	הַשַּׁבָּת הַזֶּה,

and be pleased to strengthen us on this Shabbos

on Rosh Chodesh

v'zochraynu l'tōvoh b'yōm	וְזָכְרֵנוּ לְטוֹבָה בְּיוֹם
rōsh hachōdesh hazeh,	רֹאשׁ הַחֹדֶשׁ הַזֶּה,

and be mindful of us on this holiday of the New Month

on Pesach

v'samchaynu b'yōm	וְשַׂמְּחֵנוּ בְּיוֹם
chag hamatzōs hazeh,	חַג הַמַּצּוֹת הַזֶּה,

v'samchaynu b'yōm

וְשַׂמְּחֵנוּ בְּיוֹם

chag hasukōs hazeh,

חַג הַסֻּכּוֹת הַזֶּה,

v'samchaynu b'yōm

וְשַׂמְּחֵנוּ בְּיוֹם

chag hashovu-ōs hazeh,

חַג הַשָּׁבֻעוֹת הַזֶּה,

v'samchaynu ba-yōm hashmini,

וְשַׂמְּחֵנוּ בַּיּוֹם הַשְּׁמִינִי,

chag ho-atzeres hazeh,

חַג הָעֲצֶרֶת הַזֶּה,

and let us be happy on this Festival Day of Passover/Shavuos/Sukkos/ Sh'mini Atzeres

v'zochraynu l'tōvoh b'yōm

וְזָכְרֵנוּ לְטוֹבָה בְּיוֹם

hazikorōn hazeh,

הַזִּכָּרוֹן הַזֶּה,

and remember us for good on this Day of Remembrance

ki atoh adōnoy tōv umaytiv

כִּי אַתָּה יְיָ טוֹב וּמֵטִיב

lakōl, v'nōdeh l'cho

לַכֹּל, וְנוֹדֶה לְּךָ

al ho-oretz

עַל הָאָרֶץ

for You, Lord, are good and You do good to all, and we thank You for the land

for grain products

v'al hamichyoh.

וְעַל הַמִּחְיָה.

Boruch atoh adōnoy,

בָּרוּךְ אַתָּה יְיָ,

al ho-oretz v'al hamichyoh.

עַל הָאָרֶץ וְעַל הַמִּחְיָה.

and for the sustenance. You are blessed, Lord, for the land and for the sustenance.

for fruits

v'al hapayrōs (payrōseho).

וְעַל הַפֵּרוֹת (פֵּרוֹתֶיהָ).

Boruch atoh adōnoy, al ho-oretz

בָּרוּךְ אַתָּה יְיָ, עַל הָאָרֶץ

v'al hapayrōs (payrōseho).

וְעַל הַפֵּרוֹת (פֵּרוֹתֶיהָ).

and for the fruits (its fruits). You are blessed, Lord, for the land and for the fruits (its fruits).

for wine

v'al p'ri hagofen (gafnoh).

וְעַל פְּרִי הַגָּפֶן (גַּפְנָהּ).

Boruch atoh adōnoy, al ho-oretz

בָּרוּךְ אַתָּה יְיָ, עַל הָאָרֶץ

v'al p'ri hagofen (gafnoh).

וְעַל פְּרִי הַגָּפֶן (גַּפְנָהּ).

and for the fruit of the vine (its vine). You are blessed, Lord, for the land and for the fruit of the vine (its vine).

for grain products and wine consumed together

v'al hamichyoh v'al p'ri

וְעַל הַמִּחְיָה וְעַל פְּרִי

hagofen (gafnoh). Boruch atoh

הַגָּפֶן (גַּפְנָהּ). בָּרוּךְ אַתָּה

adōnoy, al ho-oretz v'al

יְיָ, עַל הָאָרֶץ וְעַל

hamichyoh v'al p'ri

הַמִּחְיָה וְעַל פְּרִי

hagofen (gafnoh).

הַגָּפֶן (גַּפְנָהּ).

and for the sustenance and the fruit of the vine (its vine). You are blessed, Lord, for the land and the sustenance and the fruit of the vine (its vine).

(The words in parentheses are said for Israeli produce or wine.)

After food or drink not requiring either the Blessing after the Meal or the Blessing after a Snack

Boruch atoh adōnoy,

בָּרוּךְ אַתָּה יְיָ,

elōhaynu melech ho-ōlom,

אֱלֹהֵינוּ מֶלֶךְ הָעוֹלָם,

bōray n'foshōs rabōs

בּוֹרֵא נְפָשׁוֹת רַבּוֹת

v'chesrōnon, al kol mah

וְחֶסְרוֹנָן, עַל כָּל מַה

sheboroso l'hacha-yōs bohem

שֶׁבָּרֵאתָ לְהַחֲיוֹת בָּהֶם

nefesh kol choy,

נֶפֶשׁ כָּל חָי,

boruch chay ho-ōlomim.

בָּרוּךְ חֵי הָעוֹלָמִים.

You are blessed, Lord our God, the sovereign of the world, creator of many kinds of life and their needs, for everything which You created to sustain all life—You are blessed, O Eternal One.

בִּרְכַּת הַמָּזוֹן לִסְעוּדַת נְשׂוּאִין
THE BLESSING AFTER A WEDDING MEAL

Following Shir Hama-alos (page 59), at a wedding meal, and at any meal during the next six days where the bridegroom and bride and ten or more men are present, the leader takes a cup of wine and says:

Rabōsai n'voraych.　　　　　　　　　　רַבּוֹתַי נְבָרֵךְ.

My friends, let us say the blessing.

The others answer

Y'hi shaym adōnoy m'vōroch may-atoh　　יְהִי שֵׁם יְיָ מְבֹרָךְ מֵעַתָּה
v'ad ōlom.　　　　　　　　　　　　　וְעַד־עוֹלָם.

May the name of the Lord be blessed from now on and forever more.

The leader repeats

Y'hi shaym adōnoy m'vōroch may-atoh　　יְהִי שֵׁם יְיָ מְבֹרָךְ מֵעַתָּה
v'ad ōlom.　　　　　　　　　　　　　וְעַד־עוֹלָם.

May the name of the Lord be blessed from now on and forever more.

and he continues

D'vai hosayr v'gam chorōn,　　　　　דְּוַי הָסֵר וְגַם חָרוֹן,
v'oz ilaym b'shir yorōn,　　　　　　וְאָז אִלֵּם בְּשִׁיר יָרוֹן,
n'chaynu b'ma-g'lay tzedek,　　　　נְחֵנוּ בְּמַעְגְּלֵי צֶדֶק,
sh'ayh birkas b'nay aharōn.　　　　שְׁעֵה בִּרְכַּת בְּנֵי אַהֲרֹן.
Birshus moronon v'rabonon　　　　בִּרְשׁוּת מָרָנָן וְרַבָּנָן
v'rabōsai n'voraych　　　　　　　　וְרַבּוֹתַי נְבָרֵךְ
elōhaynu shehasimchoh　　　　　　אֱלֹהֵינוּ שֶׁהַשִּׂמְחָה
bim-ōnō v'she-ochalnu mishelō.　　בִּמְעוֹנוֹ וְשֶׁאָכַלְנוּ מִשֶּׁלּוֹ.

Sweep away sadness and anger, then even the dumb will cry out in song. Guide us in the paths of righteousness. Accept the blessing of the sons of Aaron. With the consent of all present, let us bless our God in whose presence the celebration is, and whose food we have eaten.

Boruch elōhaynu shehasimchoh
bim-ōnō v'she-ochalnu mishelō
uvtuvō choyinu.

בָּרוּךְ אֱלֹהֵינוּ שֶׁהַשִּׂמְחָה
בִּמְעוֹנוֹ וְשֶׁאָכַלְנוּ מִשֶּׁלּוֹ
וּבְטוּבוֹ חָיִינוּ.

Blessed is our God in whose presence the celebration is and whose food we have eaten, and through whose goodness we live.

The leader repeats

Boruch elōhaynu shehasimchoh
bim-ōnō v'she-ochalnu mishelō
uvtuvō choyinu.

בָּרוּךְ אֱלֹהֵינוּ שֶׁהַשִּׂמְחָה
בִּמְעוֹנוֹ וְשֶׁאָכַלְנוּ מִשֶּׁלּוֹ
וּבְטוּבוֹ חָיִינוּ.

Blessed is our God in whose presence the celebration is and whose food we have eaten, and through whose goodness we live.

All say

Boruch hu uvoruch sh'mō.

בָּרוּךְ הוּא וּבָרוּךְ שְׁמוֹ.

May He be blessed and may His name be blessed.

Continue on page 61.

At the conclusion of the Blessing after the Meal, the following blessings are said over a second cup of wine:

1. Boruch atoh adōnoy,
elōhaynu melech ho-ōlom,
shehakōl boro lichvōdō.

1. בָּרוּךְ אַתָּה יְיָ,
אֱלֹהֵינוּ מֶלֶךְ הָעוֹלָם,
שֶׁהַכֹּל בָּרָא לִכְבוֹדוֹ.

2. Boruch atoh adōnoy,
elōhaynu melech ho-ōlom,
yōtzayr ho-odom.

2. בָּרוּךְ אַתָּה יְיָ,
אֱלֹהֵינוּ מֶלֶךְ הָעוֹלָם,
יוֹצֵר הָאָדָם.

3. Boruch atoh adōnoy,
elōhaynu melech ho-ōlom,

3. בָּרוּךְ אַתָּה יְיָ,
אֱלֹהֵינוּ מֶלֶךְ הָעוֹלָם,

asher yotzar es ho-odom
b'tzalmō, b'tzelem d'mus
tavnisō, v'hiskin lō mimenu
binyan aday ad. Boruch atoh
adōnoy, yōtzayr ho-odom.

אֲשֶׁר יָצַר אֶת־הָאָדָם
בְּצַלְמוֹ, בְּצֶלֶם דְּמוּת
תַּבְנִיתוֹ, וְהִתְקִין לוֹ מִמֶּנּוּ
בִּנְיַן עֲדֵי עַד. בָּרוּךְ אַתָּה
יְיָ, יוֹצֵר הָאָדָם.

4. Sōs tosis v'sogayl
ho-akoroh b'kibutz boneho
l'sōchoh b'simchoh. Boruch
atoh adōnoy, m'samayach tziyōn
b'voneho.

4. שׂוֹשׂ תָּשִׂישׂ וְתָגֵל
הָעֲקָרָה בְּקִבּוּץ בָּנֶיהָ
לְתוֹכָהּ בְּשִׂמְחָה. בָּרוּךְ
אַתָּה יְיָ, מְשַׂמֵּחַ צִיּוֹן
בְּבָנֶיהָ.

5. Samayach t'samach ray-im
ho-ahuvim k'samaychacho y'tzir'cho
b'gan ayden mikedem. Boruch
atoh adōnoy, m'samayach choson
v'chaloh.

5. שַׂמֵּחַ תְּשַׂמַּח רֵעִים
הָאֲהוּבִים כְּשַׂמֵּחֲךָ יְצִירְךָ
בְּגַן עֵדֶן מִקֶּדֶם. בָּרוּךְ
אַתָּה יְיָ, מְשַׂמֵּחַ חָתָן
וְכַלָּה.

6. Boruch atoh adōnoy,
elōhaynu melech ho-ōlom,
asher boro sosōn
v'simchoh, choson v'chaloh,
giloh rinoh ditzoh v'chedvoh,
ahavoh v'achavoh v'sholōm
v'rayus. M'hayroh adōnoy elōhaynu
yishoma b'oray y'hudoh
uvchutzōs y'rushola-yim kōl
sosōn v'kōl simchoh, kōl
choson v'kōl kaloh, kōl
mitzhalōs chasonim

6. בָּרוּךְ אַתָּה יְיָ,
אֱלֹהֵינוּ מֶלֶךְ הָעוֹלָם,
אֲשֶׁר בָּרָא שָׂשׂוֹן
וְשִׂמְחָה, חָתָן וְכַלָּה,
גִּילָה רִנָּה דִּיצָה וְחֶדְוָה,
אַהֲבָה וְאַחֲוָה וְשָׁלוֹם
וְרֵעוּת. מְהֵרָה יְיָ אֱלֹהֵינוּ
יִשָּׁמַע בְּעָרֵי יְהוּדָה
וּבְחוּצוֹת יְרוּשָׁלַיִם קוֹל
שָׂשׂוֹן וְקוֹל שִׂמְחָה, קוֹל
חָתָן וְקוֹל כַּלָּה, קוֹל
מִצְהֲלוֹת חֲתָנִים

maychuposom un-orim	מֵחֻפָּתָם וּנְעָרִים
mimishtayh n'ginosom.	מִמִּשְׁתֵּה נְגִינָתָם.
Boruch atoh adōnoy,	בָּרוּךְ אַתָּה יְיָ,
m'samayach choson im hakaloh.	מְשַׂמֵּחַ חָתָן עִם הַכַּלָּה.

1. You are blessed, Lord our God, the sovereign of the world, who created everything for His glory.

2. You are blessed, Lord our God, the sovereign of the world, the creator of man.

3. You are blessed, Lord our God, the sovereign of the world, who created man in His image, in the pattern of His own likeness, and provided for the perpetuation of his kind. You are blessed, Lord, the creator of man.

4. Let the barren city be jubilantly happy and joyful at her joyous reunion with her children. You are blessed, Lord, who makes Zion rejoice with her children.

5. Let the loving couple be very happy, just as You made Your creation happy in the garden of Eden, so long ago. You are blessed, Lord, who makes the bridegroom and the bride happy.

6. You are blessed, Lord our God, the sovereign of the world, who created joy and celebration, bridegroom and bride, rejoicing, jubilation, pleasure and delight, love and brotherhood, peace and friendship. May there soon be heard, Lord our God, in the cities of Judea and in the streets of Jerusalem, the sound of joy and the sound of celebration, the voice of a bridegroom and the voice of a bride, the happy shouting of bridegrooms from their weddings and of young men from their feasts of song. You are blessed, Lord, who makes the bridegroom and the bride rejoice together.

The one who led the Blessing after the Meal
now takes the first cup of wine and says:

7. *Boruch atoh adōnoy,*	ז. בָּרוּךְ אַתָּה יְיָ,
elōhaynu melech ho-ōlom,	אֱלֹהֵינוּ מֶלֶךְ הָעוֹלָם,
bōray p'ri hagofen.	בּוֹרֵא פְּרִי הַגָּפֶן.

7. You are blessed, Lord our God, the sovereign of the world, creator of the fruit of the vine.

Wine from each of the two cups is poured into a third, empty cup. Then some wine from the third cup is poured back into each of the first two cups. One cup is given to the bridegroom to drink, one cup is given to the bride, and one to the leader.

בִּרְכַּת הַמָּזוֹן לִבְרִית מִילָה
THE BLESSING AFTER THE MEAL
FOLLOWING A CIRCUMCISION

Begin with Shir Hama-alos on page 59, then the leader continues here:

Rabōsai n'voraych.

רַבּוֹתַי נְבָרֵךְ.

My friends, let us say the blessing.

The others answer

Y'hi shaym adōnoy m'vōroch may-atoh v'ad ōlom.

יְהִי שֵׁם יְיָ מְבֹרָךְ מֵעַתָּה וְעַד־עוֹלָם.

May the name of the Lord be blessed from now on and forever more.

The leader repeats

Y'hi shaym adōnoy m'vōroch may-atoh v'ad ōlom.

יְהִי שֵׁם יְיָ מְבֹרָךְ מֵעַתָּה וְעַד־עוֹלָם.

May the name of the Lord be blessed from now on and forever more.

and he continues

Nōdeh l'shimcho b'sōch emunoy, b'ruchim atem ladōnoy.

נוֹדֶה לְשִׁמְךָ בְּתוֹךְ אֱמוּנַי, בְּרוּכִים אַתֶּם לַיְיָ.

We give thanks to Your name among the faithful; you are blessed by the Lord.

The others repeat

Nōdeh l'shimcho b'sōch emunoy, b'ruchim atem ladōnoy.

נוֹדֶה לְשִׁמְךָ בְּתוֹךְ אֱמוּנַי, בְּרוּכִים אַתֶּם לַיְיָ.

We give thanks to Your name among the faithful; you are blessed by the Lord.

Leader

Birshus ayl oyōm v'nōro,
misgov l'itōs batzoroh,
ayl ne-zor bigvuroh, adir
bamorōm adōnoy.

בִּרְשׁוּת אֵל אָיוֹם וְנוֹרָא,
מִשְׂגָּב לְעִתּוֹת בַּצָּרָה,
אֵל נֶאְזָר בִּגְבוּרָה, אַדִּיר
בַּמָרוֹם יְיָ.

With the consent of the revered and awesome God, who is a tower of strength in times of trouble; God who is girded with power, the Lord who is mighty on high.

All say

Nōdeh l'shimcho b'sōch
emunoy, b'ruchim atem ladōnoy.

נוֹדֶה לְשִׁמְךָ בְּתוֹךְ
אֱמוּנָי, בְּרוּכִים אַתֶּם לַייָ.

We give thanks to Your name among the faithful; you are blessed by the Lord.

Leader

Birshus hatōrah
hakdōshoh, t'hōroh hi
v'gam p'rushoh, tzivoh lonu
mōroshoh, mōsheh eved adōnoy.

בִּרְשׁוּת הַתּוֹרָה
הַקְּדוֹשָׁה, טְהוֹרָה הִיא
וְגַם פְּרוּשָׁה, צִוָּה לָנוּ
מוֹרָשָׁה, מֹשֶׁה עֶבֶד יְיָ.

With the consent of the holy, pure and clear Torah, which Moses, the Lord's servant, gave us as a heritage.

All say

Nōdeh l'shimcho b'sōch
emunoy, b'ruchim atem ladōnoy.

נוֹדֶה לְשִׁמְךָ בְּתוֹךְ
אֱמוּנָי, בְּרוּכִים אַתֶּם לַייָ.

We give thanks to Your name among the faithful; you are blessed by the Lord.

Leader

Birshus hakōhanim halviyim,
ekro laylōhay ho-ivriyim,

בִּרְשׁוּת הַכֹּהֲנִים הַלְוִיִּם,
אֶקְרָא לֵאלֹהֵי הָעִבְרִיִּים,

ahōdenu b'chol iyim,
avorchoh es adōnoy.

אֲהוֹדֶנוּ בְּכָל־אִיִּם,
אֲבָרְכָה אֶת־יְיָ.

With the consent of the priests, the Levites, I will call to the God of the Hebrews. I will extol Him in all the far-flung lands; I will bless the Lord.

All say

Nōdeh l'shimcho b'sōch
emunoy, b'ruchim atem ladōnoy.

נוֹדֶה לְשִׁמְךָ בְּתוֹךְ
אֱמוּנַי, בְּרוּכִים אַתֶּם לַייָ.

We give thanks to Your name among the faithful; you are blessed by the Lord.

Leader

Birshus mōrai v'rabōsai,
eftach b'shir pi usfosai,
v'sōmarnoh atzmōsai, boruch
habo b'shaym adōnoy.

בִּרְשׁוּת מוֹרַי וְרַבּוֹתַי,
אֶפְתַּח בְּשִׁיר פִּי וּשְׂפָתַי,
וְתֹאמַרְנָה עַצְמוֹתַי, בָּרוּךְ
הַבָּא בְּשֵׁם יְיָ.

With the consent of all present I will open my mouth, my lips in song, and let my whole being declare: Blessed is he who comes in the name of the Lord!

All say

Nōdeh l'shimcho b'sōch
emunoy, b'ruchim atem ladōnoy.

נוֹדֶה לְשִׁמְךָ בְּתוֹךְ
אֱמוּנַי, בְּרוּכִים אַתֶּם לַייָ.

We give thanks to Your name among the faithful; you are blessed by the Lord.

The leader continues

Birshus moronon v'rabonon
v'rabōsai n'voraych

בִּרְשׁוּת מָרָנָן וְרַבָּנָן
וְרַבּוֹתַי נְבָרֵךְ

If there are ten men present he adds

elōhaynu אֱלֹהֵינוּ

87

she-ochalnu mishelō. שָׁאָכַלְנוּ מִשֶּׁלוֹ.

With the consent of all present, let us bless him (our God) whose food we have eaten.

The others say

Boruch (elōhaynu) she-ochalnu בָּרוּךְ (אֱלֹהֵינוּ) שָׁאָכַלְנוּ
mishelō uvtuvō choyinu. מִשֶּׁלוֹ וּבְטוּבוֹ חָיִינוּ.

Blessed is He (our God) whose food we have eaten and through whose goodness we live.

The leader repeats

Boruch (elōhaynu) she-ochalnu בָּרוּךְ (אֱלֹהֵינוּ) שָׁאָכַלְנוּ
mishelō uvtuvō choyinu. מִשֶּׁלוֹ וּבְטוּבוֹ חָיִינוּ.

All say

Boruch hu uvoruch sh'mō. בָּרוּךְ הוּא וּבָרוּךְ שְׁמוֹ.

May He be blessed and may His name be blessed.

Continue with the Blessing After the Meal on page 61
until בעיני אלהים ואדם on page 73 . Then the leader continues:

1. *Horachamon hu y'voraych* א. הָרַחֲמָן הוּא יְבָרֵךְ
avi hayeled v'imō, v'yizku אֲבִי הַיֶּלֶד וְאִמּוֹ, וְיִזְכּוּ
l'gadlō ulchakmō, miyōm לְגַדְּלוֹ וּלְחַכְּמוֹ, מִיּוֹם
hashmini vohol-oh yayrotzeh הַשְּׁמִינִי וָהָלְאָה יֵרָצֶה
domō, vihi adōnoy elōhov imō. דָמוֹ, וִיהִי יְיָ אֱלֹהָיו עִמּוֹ.

May the Merciful One bless the child's father and mother and permit them to raise him, educate him and teach him wisdom. From this eighth day on may his blood be accepted, and may the Lord his God be with him.

2. *Horachamon hu y'voraych*
ba-al b'ris hamiloh, asher
sos la'sōs tzedek b'giloh,
vishalaym po-olō umaskurtō
k'fuloh, v'yitnayhu l'ma-loh
l'mo-loh.

.2 הָרַחֲמָן הוּא יְבָרֵךְ
בַּעַל בְּרִית הַמִּילָה, אֲשֶׁר
שָׂשׂ לַעֲשׂוֹת צֶדֶק בְּגִילָה,
וִישַׁלֵּם פָּעֳלוֹ וּמַשְׂכֻּרְתּוֹ
כְּפוּלָה, וְיִתְּנֵהוּ לְמַעְלָה
לְמָעְלָה.

May the Merciful One bless the *sandek* who was happy to perform this righteous act; may He reward his efforts in double measure and exalt him more and more.

3. *Horachamon hu y'voraych rach*
hanimōl lishmōnoh, v'yihyu
yodov v'libō l'ayl emunoh,
v'yizkeh lir-ōs p'nay
hashchinoh, sholōsh p'omim
bashonoh.

.3 הָרַחֲמָן הוּא יְבָרֵךְ רַךְ
הַנִּמּוֹל לִשְׁמוֹנָה, וְיִהְיוּ
יָדָיו וְלִבּוֹ לְאֵל אֱמוּנָה,
וְיִזְכֶּה לִרְאוֹת פְּנֵי
הַשְּׁכִינָה, שָׁלֹשׁ פְּעָמִים
בַּשָּׁנָה.

May the Merciful One bless the tender eight day-old infant who was circumcised; may his hands and his heart be faithful to God. May he be worthy to appear in the divine presence three times a year.

4. *Horachamon hu y'voraych*
hamol b'sar ho-orloh, ufora
umotzatz d'may hamiloh, ish
hayoray v'rach halayvov avōdosō
p'suloh, im sh'losh ayleh
lō ya-aseh loh.

.4 הָרַחֲמָן הוּא יְבָרֵךְ
הַמָּל בְּשַׂר הָעָרְלָה, וּפָרַע
וּמָצַץ דְּמֵי הַמִּילָה, אִישׁ
הַיָּרֵא וְרַךְ הַלֵּבָב עֲבוֹדָתוֹ
פְּסוּלָה, אִם שְׁלֹשׁ־אֵלֶּה
לֹא יַעֲשֶׂה לָהּ.

May the Merciful One bless the *mohel* who performed the circumcision, split the membrane and drew off some blood. The efforts of a timid or faint-hearted man who did not perform these three steps would be invalid.

5. *Horachamon hu yishlach*
lonu m'shichō hōlaych tomim,
bizchus chasnay mulōs
domim, l'vasayr b'sōrōs
tōvōs v'nichumim, l'am
echod m'fuzor umfōrod bayn
ho-amim.

5. הָרַחֲמָן הוּא יִשְׁלַח
לָנוּ מְשִׁיחוֹ הוֹלֵךְ תָּמִים,
בִּזְכוּת חַתְנֵי מוּלוֹת
דָּמִים, לְבַשֵּׂר בְּשׂוֹרוֹת
טוֹבוֹת וְנִחוּמִים, לְעַם
אֶחָד מְפֻזָּר וּמְפֹרָד בֵּין
הָעַמִּים.

May the Merciful One send us his faultless Messiah, in the merit of those related by circumcision, to bring good tidings and comfort to the unique people, scattered and dispersed among the nations.

6. *Horachamon hu yishlach*
lonu kōhayn tzedek asher lukach
l'aylōm, ad huchan kis-ō
kashemesh v'yohalōm, va-yolet
ponov b'adartō va-yiglōm,
b'risi hoysoh itō hacha-yim
v'hasholōm.

6. הָרַחֲמָן הוּא יִשְׁלַח
לָנוּ כֹּהֵן צֶדֶק אֲשֶׁר לֻקַּח
לְעֵילוֹם, עַד הוּכַן כִּסְאוֹ
כַּשֶּׁמֶשׁ וְיָהֲלוֹם, וַיָּלֶט
פָּנָיו בְּאַדַּרְתּוֹ וַיִּגְלוֹם,
בְּרִיתִי הָיְתָה אִתּוֹ הַחַיִּים
וְהַשָּׁלוֹם.

May the Merciful One send us the righteous priest who remains unseen until his shining and sparkling throne is ready; he who enveloped himself in his mantle; he who has God's covenant of life and peace.

Continue with הרחמן **on page 73 or 74 to the end of the Blessing After the meal.**

סֵדֶר בְּרָכוֹת
BLESSINGS FOR ALL OCCASIONS

As a general rule, the blessing is said before doing the action or enjoying the benefit to which it refers.

בִּרְכוֹת הַנֶּהֱנִין
Blessing for the Enjoyment of Various Benefits

בָּרוּךְ אַתָּה יְיָ, אֱלֹהֵינוּ מֶלֶךְ הָעוֹלָם,

Boruch atoh adōnoy, elōhaynu melech ho-ōlom,

You are blessed, Lord our God, the sovereign of the world,

for bread

hamōtzi lechem min ho-oretz.   הַמּוֹצִיא לֶחֶם מִן הָאָרֶץ.

who brings forth bread from the earth.

for cake, cookies, cereals, etc.

bōray minay m'zōnōs.   בּוֹרֵא מִינֵי מְזוֹנוֹת.

creator of various kinds of foods.

for fruit that grows on trees

bōray p'ri ho-aytz.   בּוֹרֵא פְּרִי הָעֵץ.

creator of the fruit of trees.

for fruits and vegetables that grow in the ground

bōray p'ri ho-adomoh.   בּוֹרֵא פְּרִי הָאֲדָמָה.

creator of the fruit of the earth.

for wine

bōray p'ri hagofen.   בּוֹרֵא פְּרִי הַגָּפֶן.

creator of the fruit of the vine.

shehakōl nihyeh bidvorō.

שֶׁהַכֹּל נִהְיֶה בִּדְבָרוֹ.

by whose word everything came into being.

bōray minay v'somim.

בּוֹרֵא מִינֵי בְשָׂמִים.

creator of various kinds of spices.

asher yotzar es ho-odom

אֲשֶׁר יָצַר אֶת־הָאָדָם

b'chochmoh, uvoro vō n'kovim

בְּחָכְמָה, וּבָרָא בוֹ נְקָבִים

n'kovim, chalulim chalulim.

נְקָבִים, חֲלוּלִים חֲלוּלִים.

Golui v'yodua lifnay chisay

גָּלוּי וְיָדוּעַ לִפְנֵי כִסֵּא

ch'vōdecho, she-im yiposayach echod

כְבוֹדֶךָ, שֶׁאִם יִפָּתֵחַ אֶחָד

mayhem ō yisosaym echod

מֵהֶם אוֹ יִסָּתֵם אֶחָד

mayhem i efshor l'hiska-yaym

מֵהֶם אִי אֶפְשָׁר לְהִתְקַיֵּם

v'la-amōd l'fonecho. Boruch

וְלַעֲמוֹד לְפָנֶיךָ. בָּרוּךְ

atoh adōnoy, rōfay chol bosor

אַתָּה יְיָ, רוֹפֵא כָל־בָּשָׂר

umafli la-asōs.

וּמַפְלִיא לַעֲשׂוֹת.

who formed man cleverly, and created in him many different organs and
channels. It is clearly evident before Your glorious throne that, should one
of these be wrongly opened, or one of them be wrongly blocked, it would be
impossible to continue to stand before You. You are blessed, Lord, who heals
all flesh in a wonderful way.

בְּרְכוֹת הַמִּצְווֹת

Blessings on the Observance of Various Commandments

בָּרוּךְ אַתָּה יְיָ, אֱלֹהֵינוּ מֶלֶךְ הָעוֹלָם,
אֲשֶׁר קִדְּשָׁנוּ בְּמִצְוֹתָיו וְצִוָּנוּ

Boruch atoh adōnoy, elōhaynu melech ho-ōlom,

asher kidshonu b'mitzvōsov v'tzivonu

You are blessed, Lord our God, the sovereign of the world,
who made us holy with His commandments and commanded us

after washing the hands prior to eating bread

al n'tilas yodoyim.   עַל נְטִילַת יָדָיִם.

to wash our hands.

before putting on the arba kanfos

al mitzvas tzitzis.   עַל מִצְוַת צִיצִית.

to wear *tzitzis*.

before putting on a tallis

l'his-atayf batzitzis.   לְהִתְעַטֵּף בַּצִּיצִית.

to enwrap ourselves with the *tzitzis*.

on putting up a mezuzah

likbō-a m'zuzoh.   לִקְבּוֹעַ מְזוּזָה.

to put up a *mezuzah*.

on immersing dishes, etc., in a mikveh

al t'vilas kaylim (keli).   עַל טְבִילַת כֵּלִים (כֶּלִי).

to immerse vessels (a vessel) in a *mikveh*.

בְּרְכוֹת רְאִיָּה וּשְׁמִיעָה
Blessings of Witnessing and Experiencing

בָּרוּךְ אַתָּה יְיָ, אֱלֹהֵינוּ מֶלֶךְ הָעוֹלָם,

Boruch atoh adōnoy, elōhaynu melech ho-ōlom,

You are blessed, Lord our God, the sovereign of the world,

on seeing lightning and other astonishing natural phenomena

ōseh ma-asayh v'rayshis.

עֹשֶׂה מַעֲשֵׂה בְרֵאשִׁית.

who performs the work of creation.

on hearing thunder, or experiencing earthquakes or tornados

shekōchō ugvurosō
molay ōlom.

שֶׁכֹּחוֹ וּגְבוּרָתוֹ
מָלֵא עוֹלָם.

whose power and might fill the world.

on seeing a rainbow

zōchayr habris v'ne-emon
bivrisō v'ka-yom b'ma-amorō.

זוֹכֵר הַבְּרִית וְנֶאֱמָן
בִּבְרִיתוֹ וְקַיָּם בְּמַאֲמָרוֹ.

who remembers the covenant, fulfills His pledge and keeps His word.

on seeing the ocean for the first time in thirty days

she-osoh es ha-yom hagodōl.

שֶׁעָשָׂה אֶת־הַיָּם הַגָּדוֹל.

who made the great ocean.

on seeing trees blossom for the first time each year

shelō chisar b'ōlomō dovor
uvoro vō b'riyōs tōvōs
v'ilonōs tōvim l'hanōs
bohem b'nay odom.

שֶׁלֹּא חִסַּר בְּעוֹלָמוֹ דָּבָר
וּבָרָא בוֹ בְּרִיּוֹת טוֹבוֹת
וְאִילָנוֹת טוֹבִים לְהַנּוֹת
בָּהֶם בְּנֵי אָדָם.

who let nothing lack from His world, but created in it beautiful creatures and lovely trees for people to enjoy.

on seeing an especially beautiful person, animal or plant

shekochoh lō b'ōlomō.

שֶׁכָּכָה לוֹ בְּעוֹלָמוֹ.

who has such phenomena in His world.

on seeing a deformed person or a monstrous creature

m'shaneh habriyōs.

מְשַׁנֶּה הַבְּרִיוֹת.

who varies the forms of His creatures.

on seeing an outstanding Torah scholar

shecholak maychochmosō liray-ov.

שֶׁחָלַק מֵחָכְמָתוֹ לִירֵאָיו.

who allots some of His wisdom to those who revere Him.

on seeing an outstanding scholar of secular subjects

shenosan maychochmosō
l'vosor vodom.

שֶׁנָּתַן מֵחָכְמָתוֹ
לְבָשָׂר וָדָם.

who gives of His wisdom to men of flesh and blood.

on seeing a Jewish king or head of state

shecholak mikvōdō liray-ov.

שֶׁחָלַק מִכְּבוֹדוֹ לִירֵאָיו.

who allots some of His glory to those who revere Him.

on seeing a non-Jewish king or head of state

shenosan mikvōdō
l'vosor vodom.

שֶׁנָּתַן מִכְּבוֹדוֹ
לְבָשָׂר וָדָם.

who gives of His glory to men of flesh and blood.

on seeing a place where miracles occurred for Israel

she-osoh nisim la-avōsaynu
bamokōm hazeh.

שֶׁעָשָׂה נִסִּים לַאֲבוֹתֵינוּ
בַּמָּקוֹם הַזֶּה.

who performed miracles for our ancestors in this place.

on seeing a place where one had personally experienced a miracle

she-osoh li nays
bamokōm hazeh.

שֶׁעָשָׂה לִי נֵס
בַּמָּקוֹם הַזֶּה.

who performed a miracle for me in this place.

on hearing very good news shared by two or more people

hatōv v'hamaytiv.

הַטּוֹב וְהַמֵּטִיב.

who is good and who does good.

on hearing very bad news

dayon ho-emes.

דַּיָּן הָאֱמֶת.

the true judge.

on purchasing a new home, new furniture, clothes, etc.; on eating a fruit for the first time in the season; and on seeing a close friend after a lapse of thirty days or more

shehecheyonu v'kiymonu v'higi-onu
lazman hazeh.

שֶׁהֶחֱיָנוּ וְקִיְּמָנוּ וְהִגִּיעָנוּ
לַזְמַן הַזֶּה.

who has kept us alive and sustained us and enabled us to reach this occasion.

שירי עם

Popular Songs

LIST OF SONGS

Achas sho-alti	5	L'ma-an achai	53
Achaynu kol bays yisro-ayl	4	Lō olecho… Shiyiboneh	49
Al ayleh	63	L'shonoh habo-oh	54
Am yisro-ayl chai	65	Mah tōvu	55
Ani ma-amin	10	M'hayroh	56
Asher boro	11	Min hamaytzar	58
Atoh hor-ayso loda-as	12	Mōdeh ani l'fonecho	57
Av horachamim	1	Na-ar hoyisi	59
Aylecho hashem ekro	8	Ōd yishoma	62
Ayleh vorechev	6	Ōmdōs hoyu raglaynu	64
Aytz cha-yim	66	Ono b'chōach	9
Bilvovi	13	Ovinu malkaynu	2
Boruch elokaynu	14	Pis-chu li	67
Boruch hagever	15	Rabōs machashovōs	70
Boruch hamokōm	16	Sh'ma b'ni	74
Chonaynu hashem chonaynu	34	Sh'ma yisro-ayl	75
Dovid melech	17	Shabchi y'rushola-yim	72
Even mo-asu	3	Shifchi chama-yim	76
Hal'lu es hashem	20	Shiroh chadoshoh	73
Hamaloch hagō-ayl	21	Simon tōv	60
Havayn yakir li	18	S'u sh'orim	71
Hinayh kayl y'shu-osi	22	Tachas asher kinay	78
Hinayh mah tōv	24	Tōras hashem	77
Hinayh yomim bo-im	23	Tōv L'hōdōs	35
Hōshi-oh es amecho	19	Tzavayh	68
Ivdu	61	Tziyōn	69
Kayl hahodo-ōs	7	Ur-ayh vonim	32
Kaytzad m'rakdim	47	Ush'avtem ma-yim	33
Ki haym cha-yaynu	43	Vaihi vishurun melech	26
Ki kayl pō-ayl	41	V'chol ma-aminim	28
Ki l'cho	45	V'ho-ayr aynaynu	25
Ki lo yitōsh	44	V'korayv p'zuraynu	31
Ki mitziyōn	46	V'lirushola-yim ircho	29
Ki v'simchoh	42	V'olu mōshi-im	30
Kōh omar hashem	40	Y'vorech'cho	36
Kol ho-ōlom	48	V'ya-azōr v'yogen	27
Layv tohōr	50	Yism'chu hashoma-yim	38
L'cho hashem hagduloh	51	Yisro-ayl b'tach	39
L'chu vonim	52	Yosis ola-yich	37

1 Av horachamim

אב הרחמים

Av horachamim shŏchayn
m'rŏmim b'rachamov
ho-atzumim hu yifkŏd
b'rachamim…Yizk'raym
elŏkaynu l'tŏvoh im sh'or
tzadikay ŏlom.

אַב הָרַחֲמִים שׁוֹכֵן
מְרוֹמִים בְּרַחֲמָיו
הָעֲצוּמִים הוּא יִפְקֹד
בְּרַחֲמִים . . . יִזְכְּרֵם
אֱלֹקֵינוּ לְטוֹבָה עִם שְׁאָר
צַדִּיקֵי עוֹלָם.

May the merciful Father who dwells on high in His overwhelming mercy call to mind our martyrs…. May he remember them favorably among the world's righteous people.

2 Ovinu malkaynu

אבינו מלכנו

Ovinu malkaynu chonaynu va-anaynu
ki ayn bonu ma-asim, asayh
imonu tz'dokoh vochesed
v'hŏshi-aynu.

אָבִינוּ מַלְכֵּנוּ חָנֵּנוּ וַעֲנֵנוּ
כִּי אֵין בָּנוּ מַעֲשִׂים, עֲשֵׂה
עִמָּנוּ צְדָקָה וָחֶסֶד
וְהוֹשִׁיעֵנוּ.

Our father, our King, be gracious to us and answer us, for we have no achievements. Deal with us charitably and kindly, and save us.

3 Even mo-asu

אבן מאסו

Even mo-asu habŏnim hoysoh
l'rŏsh pinoh. May-ays hashem
hoysoh zŏs, hi niflos
b'aynaynu.

אֶבֶן מָאֲסוּ הַבּוֹנִים הָיְתָה
לְרֹאשׁ פִּנָּה. מֵאֵת ה׳
הָיְתָה זֹּאת, הִיא נִפְלָאת
בְּעֵינֵינוּ.

The stone which the builders rejected has become the cornerstone. This is the Lord's doing, it is an amazing sight to us.

4 Achaynu kol bays yisro-ayl

אחינו כל-בית ישראל

Achaynu kol bays yisro-ayl,
han'sunim b'tzoroh uv'shivyoh,

אַחֵינוּ כָּל-בֵּית יִשְׂרָאֵל,
הַנְּתוּנִים בְּצָרָה וּבְשִּׁבְיָה,

ho-ōm'dim bayn ba-yom uvayn	הָעוֹמְדִים בֵּין בַּיָּם וּבֵין
ba-yaboshoh, hamokōm y'rachaym	בַּיַּבָּשָׁה, הַמָּקוֹם יְרַחֵם
alayhem v'yōtzi-aym mitzoroh	עֲלֵיהֶם וְיוֹצִיאֵם מִצָּרָה
lirvochoh, umay-afayloh l'ōroh,	לִרְוָחָה, וּמֵאֲפֵלָה לְאוֹרָה,
umishibud lig'ulah,	וּמִשִּׁעְבּוּד לִגְאֻלָּה,
hashto ba-agolo uvizman koriv.	הַשְׁתָּא בַּעֲגָלָא וּבִזְמַן קָרִיב.

If any of our brethren, members of the house of Israel, find themselves in trouble or in captivity, whether they are at sea or on dry land, may God take pity on them and deliver them from their trouble to well-being, from darkness to light, from captivity to freedom, now—swiftly—soon!

5 Achas sho-alti
אחת שאלתי

Achas sho-alti may-ays hashem,	אַחַת שָׁאַלְתִּי מֵאֵת ה',
ōsoh avakaysh. Shivti b'vays	אוֹתָהּ אֲבַקֵּשׁ. שִׁבְתִּי
hashem kol y'may cha-yai	בְּבֵית ה' כָּל-יְמֵי חַיַּי,
lachazōs b'nō-am hashem	לַחֲזוֹת בְּנֹעַם ה'
ulvakayr b'haycholō.	וּלְבַקֵּר בְּהֵיכָלוֹ.

There is one thing that I ask of the Lord, one thing that I desire—that I might dwell in the house of the Lord all the days of my life, witnessing the Lord's goodness and contemplating in His sanctuary.

6 Ayleh vorechev
אלה ברכב

Ayleh vorechev v'ayleh	אֵלֶּה בָרֶכֶב וְאֵלֶּה
vasusim va-anachnu	בַסּוּסִים וַאֲנַחְנוּ
b'shaym hashem nazkir.	בְּשֵׁם ה' נַזְכִּיר.

Some rely on chariots, other on cavalry, but we keep our minds on the Lord.

7 Kayl hahodo-ōs
קל ההודאות

Kayl hahodo-ōs, adōn	קֵל הַהוֹדָאוֹת, אֲדוֹן
hasholōm, m'kadaysh hashabbos	הַשָּׁלוֹם, מְקַדֵּשׁ הַשַּׁבָּת

umvoraych sh'vi-i, umayniyach
bikdushoh l'am m'dushnay
ōneg, zaycher l'ma-asayh
v'rayshis.

וּמְבָרֵךְ שְׁבִיעִי, וּמֵנִיחַ
בִּקְדֻשָּׁה לְעַם מְדֻשְּׁנֵי
עֹנֶג, זֵכֶר לְמַעֲשֵׂה
בְרֵאשִׁית.

God who deserves thanks, Lord of peace who sanctifies Shabbos, blesses the seventh day, and in holiness grants rest to a people bursting with happiness, as a reminder of the Creation.

8 Aylecho hashem ekro　　אליך ה׳ אקרא

Aylecho hashem ekro, v'el hashem
es-chanon. Sh'ma hashem v'chonayni,
hashem heyayh ōzayr li.

אֵלֶיךָ ה׳ אֶקְרָא, וְאֶל ה׳
אֶתְחַנָּן. שְׁמַע ה׳ וְחָנֵּנִי,
ה׳ הֱיֵה עֹזֵר לִי.

It is to You, Lord, that I call; it is the Lord to whom I appeal. Listen. O Lord, and be good to me; Lord, be my helper.

9 Ono b'chō-ach　　אנא בכח

Ono b'chō-ach g'dulas y'mincha
tatir tz'rurah. Kabayl rinas
amcho, sagvaynu taharaynu nōra.

אָנָּא בְּכֹחַ גְּדֻלַּת יְמִינְךָ
תַּתִּיר צְרוּרָה. קַבֵּל רִנַּת
עַמְּךָ, שַׂגְּבֵנוּ טַהֲרֵנוּ נוֹרָא.

Please, with the powerful force of Your right hand, release the captive. Accept the prayerful song of Your people; strengthen us, purify us, Awesome One!

10 Ani ma-amin　　אני מאמין

Ani ma-amin b'emunoh
sh'laymoh b'vi-as hamoshi-ach,
v'af al pi sheyismamay-ah,
im kol zeh achakeh lō
b'chol yom she-yovō.

אֲנִי מַאֲמִין בֶּאֱמוּנָה
שְׁלֵמָה בְּבִיאַת הַמָּשִׁיחַ,
וְאַף עַל פִּי שֶׁיִּתְמַהְמֵהַּ,
עִם כָּל־זֶה אֲחַכֶּה לוֹ
בְּכָל־יוֹם שֶׁיָּבֹא.

I believe with perfect faith that the Messiah will come; and even though he may take his time, I will expect his arrival each and every day.

11 Asher boro

אשר ברא

Asher boro sosōn
v'simchoh, choson v'chaloh,
giloh rinoh ditzoh v'chedvoh,
ahavoh v'achavoh, v'sholōm
v'rayus. M'hayroh hashem elōkaynu
yishoma b'oray y'hudoh
uvchutzōs y'rushola-yim
kol sosōn v'kol simchoh,
kol choson v'kol kaloh.

אֲשֶׁר בָּרָא שָׂשׂוֹן
וְשִׂמְחָה, חָתָן וְכַלָּה,
גִּילָה רִנָּה דִּיצָה וְחֶדְוָה,
אַהֲבָה וְאַחֲוָה, וְשָׁלוֹם
וְרֵעוּת. מְהֵרָה ה' אֱלֹקֵינוּ
יִשָּׁמַע בְּעָרֵי יְהוּדָה
וּבְחוּצוֹת יְרוּשָׁלַיִם
קוֹל שָׂשׂוֹן וְקוֹל שִׂמְחָה,
קוֹל חָתָן וְקוֹל כַּלָּה.

Blessed is He who created joy and celebration, bridegroom and bride, rejoicing, jubilation, pleasure and delight, love and brotherhood, peace and friendship. May there soon be heard, Lord our God, in the cities of Judea and in the streets of Jerusalem, the sound of joy and the sound of celebration, the voice of a bridegroom and the voice of a bride.

12 Atoh horayso loda-as

אתה הראת לדעת

Atoh horayso loda-as ki hashem
hu ho-elōkim, ayn ōd milvadō.

אַתָּה הָרְאֵתָ לָדַעַת כִּי ה'
הוּא הָאֱלֹקִים, אֵין עוֹד מִלְבַדּוֹ.

You were instructed that the Lord, He is God; there is no other besides Him.

13 Bilvovi

בלבבי

Bilvovi mishkon evneh,
lahadar k'vōdō, uvamishkon
mizbayach osim, l'karnay
hōdō. Ul'nayr tomid ekach
li, es aysh ho-akaydoh,
ulkorbon akriv lō es
nafshi ha-y'chidoh.

בִּלְבָבִי מִשְׁכָּן אֶבְנֶה,
לַהֲדַר כְּבוֹדוֹ, וּבַמִּשְׁכָּן
מִזְבֵּחַ אָשִׂים, לְקַרְנֵי
הוֹדוֹ. וּלְנֵר תָּמִיד אֶקַּח
לִי, אֶת־אֵשׁ הָעֲקֵדָה,
וּלְקָרְבָּן אַקְרִיב לוֹ אֶת־
נַפְשִׁי הַיְחִידָה.

In my heart I will erect a sanctuary to glorify His honor, and in the sanctuary I will place an altar to the glories of His splendor. For the eternal light I will take the fire of the Akedah, and for a sacrifice I will offer my soul, my unique soul.

14 Boruch elōkaynu

ברוך אלקינו

Boruch elōkaynu shebro-onu lichvōdō, v'hivdilonu min hatō-im, v'nosan lonu toras emes, v'cha-yay ōlom nota b'sōchaynu.

בָּרוּךְ אֱלֹקֵינוּ שֶׁבְּרָאָנוּ לִכְבוֹדוֹ, וְהִבְדִּילָנוּ מִן הַתּוֹעִים, וְנָתַן לָנוּ תּוֹרַת אֱמֶת, וְחַיֵּי עוֹלָם נָטַע בְּתוֹכֵנוּ.

Blessed is our God who created us for His glory, who set us apart from those who miss the mark, who gave us the Torah of truth, and who planted eternal life in our midst.

15 Boruch hagever

ברוך הגבר

Boruch hagever asher yivtach bashem, v'hoyoh hashem mivtachō.

בָּרוּךְ הַגֶּבֶר אֲשֶׁר יִבְטַח בַּה', וְהָיָה ה' מִבְטַחוֹ.

Blessed is the man who trusts in the Lord, and who makes the Lord the object of his trust.

16 Boruch hamokōm

ברוך המקום

Boruch hamokōm boruch hu, boruch shenosan tōrah, l'amō yisro-ayl boruch hu.

בָּרוּךְ הַמָּקוֹם בָּרוּךְ הוּא, בָּרוּךְ שֶׁנָּתַן תּוֹרָה, לְעַמּוֹ יִשְׂרָאֵל, בָּרוּךְ הוּא.

Blessed is God, blessed is He. Blessed is He who gave the Torah to His people Israel; blessed is He.

17 Dovid melech

דוד מלך

Dovid melech yisro-ayl chai v'ka-yom.

דָּוִד מֶלֶךְ יִשְׂרָאֵל חַי וְקַיָּם.

David, King of Israel, lives forever.

18 Havayn yakir li

הבן יקיר

Havayn yakir li efra-yim, im
yeled sha-ashu-im, ki miday
dabri bō zochor ezk'renu ōd.

הֲבֵן יַקִּיר לִי אֶפְרַיִם אִם
יֶלֶד שַׁעֲשׁוּעִים, כִּי מִדֵּי
דַבְּרִי בּוֹ זָכֹר אֶזְכְּרֶנּוּ עוֹד.

Is it because Ephraim is my beloved son, or that he is such a lovely child, that—whenever I mention him—I yearn for him more and more?

19 Hōshi-oh es amecho

הושיעה את־עמך

Hōshi-oh es amecho
uvoraych es nachalosecho, ur-aym
v'nas-aym ad ho-ōlom.

הוֹשִׁיעָה אֶת־עַמֶּךָ,
וּבָרֵךְ אֶת־נַחֲלָתֶךָ, וּרְעֵם
וְנַשְּׂאֵם עַד הָעוֹלָם.

Save Your people and bless Your possession; tend them and sustain them forever.

20 Hal'lu es hashem

הללו את־ה'

Hal'lu es hashem kol gōyim,
shabchuhu kol ho-umim. Ki
govar olaynu chasdō, ve-emes
hashem l'ōlom, hal'lukoh.

הַלְלוּ אֶת־ה' כָּל־גּוֹיִם,
שַׁבְּחוּהוּ כָּל־הָאֻמִּים. כִּי
גָבַר עָלֵינוּ חַסְדּוֹ, וֶאֱמֶת
ה' לְעוֹלָם, הַלְלוּיָהּ.

Praise the Lord, all nations! Salute Him, all peoples! For his kindness dominates us, and the Lord's truth is eternal; Praise the Lord!

21 Hamaloch hagō-ayl

המלאך הגאל

Hamaloch hagō-ayl ōsi mikol
ro y'vorech es han'orim,
v'yikoray vohem sh'mi v'shaym
avōsai avrohom v'yitzchok,
v'yidgu lorōv b'kerev ho-oretz.

הַמַּלְאָךְ הַגֹּאֵל אֹתִי מִכָּל־
רָע יְבָרֵךְ אֶת־הַנְּעָרִים,
וְיִקָּרֵא בָהֶם שְׁמִי וְשֵׁם
אֲבֹתַי אַבְרָהָם וְיִצְחָק,
וְיִדְגּוּ לָרֹב בְּקֶרֶב הָאָרֶץ.

May the angel who protects me from all evil bless the youngsters, and may their reputation become like mine and that of my fathers Abraham and Isaac, and may they teem in swarms in the land.

22 Hinayh kayl y'shu-osi

הנה קל ישועתי

Hinayh kayl y'shu-osi, evtach
v'lō efchod, ki ozi
v'zimros koh hashem, vaihi li
lishu-oh. Ush'avtem ma-yim
b'sosōn mima-ai-nay hai-shu-oh.
Lashem hai-shu-oh, al amcho
birchosecho seloh.

הִנֵּה קֵל יְשׁוּעָתִי, אֶבְטַח
וְלֹא אֶפְחָד, כִּי עָזִּי
וְזִמְרָת קָה ה׳, וַיְהִי לִי
לִישׁוּעָה. וּשְׁאַבְתֶּם מַיִם
בְּשָׂשׂוֹן מִמַּעַיְנֵי הַיְשׁוּעָה.
לה׳ הַיְשׁוּעָה, עַל עַמְךָ
בִרְכָתֶךָ סֶּלָה.

Behold, God is my salvation, I will have trust and not be afraid. Indeed, the Lord is my strength and my song and He has become my salvation. You should draw water with joy from the wells of salvation. Salvation belongs to the Lord; may Your blessing be upon Your people, Selah.

23 Hinayh yomim bo-im

הנה ימים באים

Hinayh yomim
bo-im…
V'hishlachti ro-ov bo-oretz,
lō ro-ov lalechem v'lō
tzomo lama-yim, ki im
lishmō-a ays divray hashem.

הִנֵּה יָמִים
בָּאִים . . .
וְהִשְׁלַחְתִּי רָעָב בָּאָרֶץ,
לֹא רָעָב לַלֶּחֶם וְלֹא
צָמָא לַמַּיִם, כִּי אִם
לִשְׁמֹעַ אֶת דִּבְרֵי ה׳.

Behold, days are coming when I will send a famine in the land; not a famine of bread, nor a thirst for water, but of learning the words of the Lord.

24 Hinayh mah-tōv

הנה מה טוב

Hinayh mah-tōv umah na-im
sheves achim gam yochad.

הִנֵּה מַה טוֹב וּמַה נָּעִים
שֶׁבֶת אַחִים גַּם יָחַד.

How good and pleasant it is when brothers live together in harmony.

25 V'ho-ayr aynaynu

 והאר עינינו

V'ho-ayr aynaynu v'sŏrosecho,
v'dabayk libaynu b'mitzvŏsecho,
v'yachayd l'vovaynu l'ahavoh
ulyir-oh es sh'mecho, shelŏ
nayvŏsh v'lŏ nikolaym v'lŏ
nikoshayl l'ŏlom vo-ed.

וְהָאֵר עֵינֵינוּ בְּתוֹרָתֶךָ,
וְדַבֵּק לִבֵּנוּ בְּמִצְוֹתֶיךָ,
וְיַחֵד לְבָבֵנוּ לְאַהֲבָה
וּלְיִרְאָה אֶת־שְׁמֶךָ, שֶׁלֹּא
נֵבוֹשׁ וְלֹא נִכָּלֵם וְלֹא
נִכָּשֵׁל לְעוֹלָם וָעֶד.

Enlighten our eyes with Your Torah, harness our hearts to Your mitzvos, and unify our resolve to love and respect Your name, so that we should never feel embarrassed or ashamed or put down.

26 Vaihi vishurun melech

ויהי בישרון מלך

Vaihi vishurun melech
b'his-asayf roshay om,
yachad shivtay yisro-ayl.

וַיְהִי בִישֻׁרוּן מֶלֶךְ
בְּהִתְאַסֵּף רָאשֵׁי עָם,
יַחַד שִׁבְטֵי יִשְׂרָאֵל.

He became King of Yeshurun when the leaders of the people assembled, when the tribes of Israel were united.

27 V'ya-azor v'yogayn

ויעזר ויגן

V'ya-azŏr v'yogayn v'yŏshi-a
l'chŏl hachŏsim bŏ.

וְיַעֲזֹר וְיָגֵן וְיוֹשִׁיעַ
לְכָל הַחוֹסִים בּוֹ.

May He help, shield and redeem all those who turn to Him for refuge.

28 V'chol ma-aminim

וכל מאמינים

V'chol ma-aminim shehu chai
v'ka-yom, hatŏv umaytiv
loro-im v'latŏvim.

וְכָל מַאֲמִינִים שֶׁהוּא חַי
וְקַיָּם, הַטּוֹב וּמֵטִיב
לָרָעִים וְלַטּוֹבִים.

Everyone acknowledges that He lives and endures; He is good and benevolent to both wicked and good people.

29 V'lirushola-yim ircho

ולירושלים עירך

V'lirushola-yim ircho
b'rachamim toshuv v'sishkōn
b'sōchoh ka-asher dibarto,
uv'nay ōsoh b'korōv
b'yomaynu binyan ōlom, v'chisay
dovid m'hayroh l'sōchoh tochin.

וְלִירוּשָׁלַיִם עִירְךָ
בְּרַחֲמִים תָּשׁוּב, וְתִשְׁכּוֹן
בְּתוֹכָהּ כַּאֲשֶׁר דִּבַּרְתָּ,
וּבְנֵה אוֹתָהּ בְּקָרוֹב
בְּיָמֵינוּ בִּנְיַן עוֹלָם, וְכִסֵּא
דָוִד מְהֵרָה לְתוֹכָהּ תָּכִין.

Return, out of compassion, to Your city Jerusalem, residing in it as You said You would; rebuild it soon in our time as an everlasting structure, and swiftly establish David's throne there.

30 V'olu mōshi-im

ועלו מושיעים

V'olu mōshi-im b'har
tziyōn lishpōt es har
aysov v'hoysoh lashem
hamluchoh. V'hoyoh hashem
l'melech al kol ho-oretz,
bayōm hahu yihyeh hashem
echod ushmō echod.

וְעָלוּ מוֹשִׁיעִים בְּהַר
צִיּוֹן לִשְׁפֹּט אֶת־הַר
עֵשָׂו וְהָיְתָה לַה׳
הַמְּלוּכָה. וְהָיָה ה׳
לְמֶלֶךְ עַל כָּל־הָאָרֶץ,
בַּיּוֹם הַהוּא יִהְיֶה ה׳
אֶחָד וּשְׁמוֹ אֶחָד.

Deliverers shall ascent Mount Zion to render judgment on Esau's mountain, and sovereignty shall belong to the Lord. The Lord will become King of the whole earth; on that day the Lord will be one and His name one.

31 V'korayv p'zuraynu

וקרב פזורינו

V'korayv p'zuraynu mibayn hagōyim
unfutzōsaynu kanays miyark'say
oretz. Vahavi-aynu l'tziyōn
ir'cho b'rinoh, v'lirushola-yim
bays mikdoshcho b'simchas
ōlom.

וְקָרֵב פְּזוּרֵינוּ מִבֵּין הַגּוֹיִם
וּנְפוּצוֹתֵינוּ כַּנֵּס מִיַּרְכְּתֵי
אָרֶץ. וַהֲבִיאֵנוּ לְצִיּוֹן
עִירְךָ בְּרִנָּה, וְלִירוּשָׁלַיִם
בֵּית מִקְדָּשְׁךָ בְּשִׂמְחַת
עוֹלָם.

Assemble our scattered people from among the nations and gather our dispersed ones from the ends of the earth. Bring us to Zion, Your city, and to Jerusalem, Your sanctuary, in eternal joy.

32 Ur-ayh vonim

וראה בנים

Ur-ayh vonim l'vonecho,
sholōm al yisro-ayl.

וּרְאֵה בָנִים לְבָנֶיךָ,
שָׁלוֹם עַל יִשְׂרָאֵל.

May you live to see your children's children. May Israel have peace!

33 Ush'avtem ma-yim

ושאבתם מים

Ush'avtem ma-yim b'sosōn
mima-ai-nay hai-shu-oh.

וּשְׁאַבְתֶּם מַיִם בְּשָׂשׂוֹן
מִמַּעַיְנֵי הַיְשׁוּעָה.

You shall draw water with joy from the wells of salvation.

34 Chonaynu hashem chonaynu

חננו ה' חננו

Chonaynu hashem chonaynu,
ki rav sova-nu vuz.

חָנֵּנוּ ה' חָנֵּנוּ,
כִּי רַב שָׂבַעְנוּ בוּז.

Be gracious to us, Lord, be gracious to us, for we have had enough of contempt.

35 Tōv l'hōdōs

טוב להודות

Tōv l'hōdōs lashem ul'zamayr
l'shimcho elyōn. L'hagid
babōker chasdecho ve-emunos-cho
balaylōs.

טוֹב לְהֹדוֹת לַה' וּלְזַמֵּר
לְשִׁמְךָ עֶלְיוֹן. לְהַגִּיד
בַּבֹּקֶר חַסְדֶּךָ וֶאֱמוּנָתְךָ
בַּלֵּילוֹת.

It is good to give thanks to the Lord, to sing praises to Your name, Exalted One; to tell of Your kindness in the morning and of Your steadfastness by night.

36 Y'vorech'cho

יברכך

Y'vorech'cho hashem mitziyōn ur-ayh
b'tuv y'rusholoyim. Y'vorech'cho
hashem mitziyōn kol y'may cha-yecho.

יְבָרֶכְךָ ה' מִצִּיּוֹן וּרְאֵה
בְּטוּב יְרוּשָׁלָיִם. יְבָרֶכְךָ
ה' מִצִּיּוֹן כֹּל יְמֵי חַיֶּיךָ.

May the Lord bless you from Zion and may you see the prosperity of Jerusalem. May the Lord bless you from Zion all the days of your life.

37 Yosis ola-yich

Yosis ola-yich elōkoyich
kimsōs choson al kaloh.

ישיש עליך

יָשִׂישׂ עָלַיִךְ אֱלֹקָיִךְ
כִּמְשׂוֹשׂ חָתָן עַל כַּלָּה.

May your God rejoice over you as a bridegroom rejoices over the bride.

38 Yism'chu hashoma-yim

Yism'chu hashoma-yim v'sogayl
ho-oretz, yir-am ha-yom
umlō-ō.

ישמחו השמים

יִשְׂמְחוּ הַשָּׁמַיִם וְתָגֵל
הָאָרֶץ, יִרְעַם הַיָּם
וּמְלֹאוֹ.

Let the heavens rejoice and the earth be glad; let the sea and all it contains thunder and praise.

39 Yisro-ayl b'tach

Yisro-ayl b'tach bashem, ezrom
umoginom hu.

ישראל בטח

יִשְׂרָאֵל בְּטַח בַּה', עֶזְרָם
וּמָגִנָּם הוּא.

Israel trusts the Lord; He is their help and protector.

40 Kōh omar hashem

Kōh omar hashem: motzo chayn
bamidbor, am s'riday chorev,
holōch l'hargi-ō yisro-ayl.

כה אמר ה'

כֹּה אָמַר ה': מָצָא חֵן
בַּמִּדְבָּר, עַם שְׂרִידֵי חָרֶב,
הָלוֹךְ לְהַרְגִּיעוֹ יִשְׂרָאֵל.

Thus says the Lord: The people who survived the sword have found grace in the wilderness; now I go to give Israel rest.

41 Ki kayl pō-ayl

Ki kayl pō-ayl y'shu-ōs
otoh uvonu vocharto mikol

כי קל פועל

כִּי קֵל פּוֹעֵל יְשׁוּעוֹת
אַתָּה וּבָנוּ בָחַרְתָּ מִכָּל־

am v'loshōn, v'kayravtonu
l'shimcho hogodōl seloh
be-emes l'hōdōs l'cho
ulyachedcho b'ahavoh
ul-ahavoh es sh'mecho.

עַם וְלָשׁוֹן, וְקֵרַבְתָּנוּ
לְשִׁמְךָ הַגָּדוֹל סֶלָה
בֶּאֱמֶת לְהוֹדוֹת לְךָ
וּלְיַחֶדְךָ בְּאַהֲבָה
וּלְאַהֲבָה אֶת־שְׁמֶךָ.

You, God, bring about salvation; You chose us out of all nations and societies and brought us truly close, our King, to Your great name, to give thanks to You, to proclaim Your unity with love, and our love for Your name.

42 Ki v'simchoh   כי בשמחה

Ki v'simchoh saytzay-u
uvsholōm tuvolun, hehorim
v'hagvo-ōs yiftz'chu lifnaychem
rinoh v'chol atzay hasodeh
yimcha-u chof.

כִּי בְשִׂמְחָה תֵצֵאוּ
וּבְשָׁלוֹם תּוּבָלוּן, הֶהָרִים
וְהַגְּבָעוֹת יִפְצְחוּ לִפְנֵיכֶם
רִנָּה וְכָל־עֲצֵי הַשָּׂדֶה
יִמְחֲאוּ־כָף.

For you will go out joyfully and be led forth peacefully. Mountains and hills will burst into song before you, and all the trees will clap.

43 Ki haym cha-yaynu   כי הם חיינו

Ki haym cha-yaynu v'ōrech
yomaynu uvohem nehgeh yōmom
voloyloh.

כִּי הֵם חַיֵּינוּ וְאֹרֶךְ יָמֵינוּ
וּבָהֶם נֶהְגֶּה יוֹמָם
וָלָיְלָה.

The mitzvos fill our lives and the length of our days, and we will study them day and night.

44 Ki lō yitōsh   כי לא יטש

Ki lō yitōsh hashem amō,
v'nachalosō lō ya-azōv. Hashem
hōshi-oh, hamelech ya-anaynu
v'yōm kor-aynu.

כִּי לֹא יִטֹּשׁ ה׳ עַמּוֹ,
וְנַחֲלָתוֹ לֹא יַעֲזֹב. ה׳
הוֹשִׁיעָה, הַמֶּלֶךְ יַעֲנֵנוּ
בְיוֹם קָרְאֵנוּ.

For the Lord will not abandon his people, nor forsake His possession. Lord, save us; may the King answer us when we call.

45 Ki l'cho

כי לך

Ki l'cho tōv l'hōdōs
ulshimcho no-eh l'zamayr, ki
may-ōlom v'ad ōlom
atoh kayl.

כִּי לְךָ טוֹב לְהוֹדוֹת
וּלְשִׁמְךָ נָאֶה לְזַמֵּר, כִּי
מֵעוֹלָם וְעַד עוֹלָם
אַתָּה קֵל.

It is good to give thanks to You and pleasant to sing praises to Your name, for You are God forever.

46 Ki mitziyōn

כי מציון

Ki mitziyōn taytzay sōroh
udvar hashem mirusholoyim.

כִּי מִצִּיּוֹן תֵּצֵא תוֹרָה
וּדְבַר ה' מִירוּשָׁלָיִם.

Torah shall emanate from Zion and the word of the Lord from Jerusalem.

47 Kaytzad m'rakdim

כיצד מרקדים

Kaytzad m'rakdim lifnay
hakaloh, kaloh no-oh
vachasudoh.

כֵּיצַד מְרַקְדִים לִפְנֵי
הַכַּלָּה, כַּלָּה נָאָה
וַחֲסוּדָה.

What does one say when dancing before a bride? "The bride is beautiful and virtuous."

48 Kol ho-ōlom

כל העולם

Kol ho-ōlom kulō gesher tzar
m'ōd v'ho-ikor lō l'fachayd
k'lol.

כָּל הָעוֹלָם כֻּלּוֹ גֶּשֶׁר צַר
מְאֹד וְהָעִיקָר לֹא לְפַחֵד
כְּלָל.

The whole world is a very narrow bridge, but what matters most is not to be at all afraid.

49 Lŏ olecho. . . She-yiboneh

Lŏ olecho hamlochoh
ligmŏr v'lŏ atoh ven
chorin l'hibotel mimenoh….
She-yiboneh bays hamikdosh
bim'hayroh v'yomaynu.

לא עליך... שיבנה

לֹא עָלֶיךָ הַמְּלָאכָה
לִגְמֹר, וְלֹא אַתָּה בֶן
חוֹרִין לְהִבָּטֵל מִמֶּנָּה...
שֶׁיִּבָּנֶה בֵּית הַמִּקְדָּשׁ
בִּמְהֵרָה בְיָמֵינוּ.

Even though it may not be your responsibility to complete the job, that does not mean that you are free to disregard it…. May the Temple be rebuilt swiftly, in our time.

50 Layv tohŏr

Layv tohŏr b'ro li
elŏkim, v'ruach nochŏn chadaysh
b'kirbi. Al tashlichayni
milfonecho v'ruach kodsh'cho
al tikach mimeni.

לב טהור

לֵב טָהוֹר בְּרָא לִי
אֱלֹקִים, וְרוּחַ נָכוֹן חַדֵּשׁ
בְּקִרְבִּי. אַל תַּשְׁלִיכֵנִי
מִלְּפָנֶיךָ וְרוּחַ קָדְשְׁךָ
אַל תִּקַּח מִמֶּנִּי.

Form a pure heart for me, God, and restore the proper spirit to me. Do not reject me and do not take Your holy spirit away from me.

51 L'cho hashem hagduloh

L'cho hashem hagduloh v'hagvuroh
v'hatif-eres v'hanaytzach
v'hahŏd, ki chol bashoma-yim
uvo-oretz. L'cho hashem hamamlochoh
v'hamisnasay l'chŏl l'rŏsh.

לך ה' הגדולה

לְךָ ה' הַגְּדוּלָה וְהַגְּבוּרָה
וְהַתִּפְאֶרֶת וְהַנֵּצַח
וְהַהוֹד, כִּי כֹל בַּשָּׁמַיִם
וּבָאָרֶץ. לְךָ ה' הַמַּמְלָכָה
וְהַמִּתְנַשֵּׂא לְכֹל לְרֹאשׁ.

Greatness, might splendor, supremacy and majesty are Yours, Lord, as is everything that is in heaven and on earth. Dominion is Yours and You are pre-eminent over all.

113

52 L'chu vonim

לכו בנים

L'chu vonim shimu li
yir-as hashem alamedchem.
Mi ho-ish hechofaytz cha-yim
ðhayv yomim lir-ōs tōv.
N'tzōr l'shōncho mayro
usfosecho midabayr mirmoh.

לְכוּ בָנִים שִׁמְעוּ לִי
יִרְאַת ה׳ אֲלַמֶּדְכֶם.
מִי הָאִישׁ הֶחָפֵץ חַיִּים
אֹהֵב יָמִים לִרְאוֹת טוֹב.
נְצֹר לְשׁוֹנְךָ מֵרָע
וּשְׂפָתֶיךָ מִדַּבֵּר מִרְמָה.

Come, children, listen to me, I am going to teach you how to respect the Lord. Who is the man who delights in life, who loves life and enjoys its bounty? Keep your tongue from evil and your lips from speaking lies.

53 L'ma-an achai

למען אחי

L'ma-an achai v'ray-oy adabroh
no sholōm boch. L'ma-an bays
hashem elōkaynu avakshoh
tōv loch.

לְמַעַן אַחַי וְרֵעָי אֲדַבְּרָה
נָּא שָׁלוֹם בָּךְ. לְמַעַן בֵּית
ה׳ אֱלֹקֵינוּ אֲבַקְשָׁה
טוֹב לָךְ.

For the sake of my brothers and friends, let me now talk of peace. For the sake of the house of the Lord our God, let me strive after good things for you.

54 L'shonoh habo-oh

לשנה הבאה

L'shonoh habo-oh
birushola-yim habnuyoh.

לְשָׁנָה הַבָּאָה
בִּירוּשָׁלַיִם הַבְּנוּיָה.

Next year may we be in rebuilt Jerusalem.

55 Mah tōvu

מה טבו

Mah tōvu ðholecho ya-akōv,
mishk'nōsecho yisro-ayl. Va-ani
b'rōv chasd'cho ovō vaysecho,
eshtachaveh el haychal
kodsh'cho b'yir-osecho.

מַה טֹּבוּ אֹהָלֶיךָ יַעֲקֹב,
מִשְׁכְּנֹתֶיךָ יִשְׂרָאֵל. וַאֲנִי
בְּרֹב חַסְדְּךָ אָבֹא בֵיתֶךָ,
אֶשְׁתַּחֲוֶה אֶל הֵיכַל
קָדְשְׁךָ בְּיִרְאָתֶךָ.

How fine are your tents, Jacob, your homes, Israel. As for me, I come to Your home through Your abundant kindness; I worship in Your holy sanctuary in awe of You.

56 M'hayroh

מהרה

M'hayroh hashem elōkaynu yishoma
b'oray y'hudoh uvchutzōs
y'rushola-yim kōl sosōn v'kōl
simchoh, kōl choson v'kōl
kaloh, kōl mitzhalōs
chasonim maychuposom un'orim
mimishtayh n'ginosom.

מְהֵרָה, ה' אֱלֹקֵינוּ, יִשָּׁמַע
בְּעָרֵי יְהוּדָה וּבְחוּצוֹת
יְרוּשָׁלַיִם קוֹל שָׂשׂוֹן וְקוֹל
שִׂמְחָה, קוֹל חָתָן וְקוֹל
כַּלָּה, קוֹל מִצְהֲלוֹת
חֲתָנִים מֵחֻפָּתָם וּנְעָרִים
מִמִּשְׁתֵּה נְגִינָתָם.

May there soon be heard, Lord our God, in the cities of Judea and in the streets of Jerusalem, the sound of joy and the sound of celebration, the voice of a bridegroom and the voice of a bride, the happy shouting of bridegrooms and of young men from their feasts of song.

57 Mōdeh ani l'fonecho

מודה אני לפניך

Mōdeh ani l'fonecho melech chai
v'ka-yom, shehechezarto bi
nishmosi b'chemloh,
raboh emunosecho.

מוֹדֶה אֲנִי לְפָנֶיךָ מֶלֶךְ חַי
וְקַיָּם, שֶׁהֶחֱזַרְתָּ בִּי
נִשְׁמָתִי בְּחֶמְלָה,
רַבָּה אֱמוּנָתֶךָ.

I acknowledge before You, everliving and everlasting King, that You have restored my soul to me in mercy; Your faithfulness is unbounded.

58 Min hamaytzar

מן המצר

Min hamaytzar korosi koh,
ononi vamerchov koh.

מִן הַמֵּצַר קָרָאתִי קָהּ,
עֲנָנִי בַמֶּרְחָב קָהּ.

From my confinement I called to God; His wide open space was His reply.

59 Na-ar ho-yisi

נער הייתי

Na-ar ho-yisi gam zokanti
v'lō ro-isi tzadik ne-ezov
v'zar'ō m'vakesh lochem.
Hashem ōz l'amō yitayn,
hashem y'voraych es amō vashōlom.

נַעַר הָיִיתִי גַּם זָקַנְתִּי,
וְלֹא רָאִיתִי צַדִּיק נֶעֱזָב,
וְזַרְעוֹ מְבַקֶּשׁ לָחֶם.
ה' עֹז לְעַמּוֹ יִתֵּן,
ה' יְבָרֵךְ אֶת־עַמּוֹ בַשָּׁלוֹם.

I was young and I have grown old, and yet I never overlooked a deserving man who was destitute, with his children begging for bread. May the Lord give strength to His people; may the Lord bless His people with peace.

60 Simon tōv

סמן טוב

Simon tōv umazol tōv y'hay
lonu ulchol yisro-ayl, omayn.

סִמָּן טוֹב וּמַזָּל טוֹב יְהֵא
לָנוּ וּלְכָל יִשְׂרָאֵל, אָמֵן.

May we and all of Israel have a good omen and good luck.

61 Ivdu

עבדו

Ivdu es hashem b'simchoh,
bō-u l'fonov birnonoh.

עִבְדוּ אֶת־ה' בְּשִׂמְחָה,
בֹּאוּ לְפָנָיו בִּרְנָנָה.

Serve the Lord with joy, come before Him with happy singing.

62 Ōd yishoma

עוד ישמע

Ōd yishoma b'oray y'hudoh
uvchutzōs y'rusholoyim, kōl
sosōn v'kōl simchoh,
kōl choson v'kōl kaloh.

עוֹד יִשָּׁמַע בְּעָרֵי יְהוּדָה
וּבְחוּצוֹת יְרוּשָׁלָיִם, קוֹל
שָׂשׂוֹן וְקוֹל שִׂמְחָה,
קוֹל חָתָן וְקוֹל כַּלָּה.

May there still be heard in the cities of Judea and in the streets of Jerusalem, the sound of joy and the sound of celebration, the voice of the bridegroom and the voice of the bride.

63 Al ayleh

עַל אֵלֶּה

Al ayleh ani vōchiyoh,
hasichyenoh ho-atzomōs ho-ayleh.

עַל אֵלֶּה אֲנִי בוֹכִיָּה,
הֲתִחְיֶינָה הָעֲצָמוֹת הָאֵלֶּה.

I cry for these things; can these bones live?

64 Ōmdos hoyu raglaynu

עֹמְדוֹת הָיוּ רַגְלֵינוּ

Ōmdos hoyu raglaynu
bish-orayich y'rushola-yim.
Y'rushola-yim habnuyoh k'ir
shechubroh loh yachdov. L'shono
habo-oh birusholoyim.

עֹמְדוֹת הָיוּ רַגְלֵינוּ
בִּשְׁעָרַיִךְ יְרוּשָׁלָיִם.
יְרוּשָׁלַיִם הַבְּנוּיָה כְּעִיר
שֶׁחֻבְּרָה־לָּהּ יַחְדָּו. לְשָׁנָה
הַבָּאָה בִּירוּשָׁלָיִם.

Our feet stood inside your gates, Jerusalem—Jerusalem that is built as a self-contained city. Next year may we be in Jerusalem!

65 Am yisro-ayl chai

עַם יִשְׂרָאֵל חַי

Am yisro-ayl chai,
ōd ovinu chai.

עַם יִשְׂרָאֵל חַי,
עוֹד אָבִינוּ חַי.

The people of Israel lives; our Father still lives!

66 Aytz cha-yim

עֵץ חַיִּים

Aytz cha-yim hi lamachazikim
boh v'sōmcheho m'ushor.
D'rocheho darchay nō-am v'chol
n'sivōseho sholōm.
Hashivaynu hashem aylecho
v'noshuvoh, chadaysh yomaynu
k'kedem.

עֵץ חַיִּים הִיא לַמַּחֲזִיקִים
בָּהּ וְתֹמְכֶיהָ מְאֻשָּׁר.
דְּרָכֶיהָ דַרְכֵי נֹעַם וְכָל־
נְתִיבוֹתֶיהָ שָׁלוֹם.
הֲשִׁיבֵנוּ ה' אֵלֶיךָ
וְנָשׁוּבָה, חַדֵּשׁ יָמֵינוּ
כְּקֶדֶם.

It is a tree of life to those who grasp it and its supporters are happy. Its ways are pleasant and its paths are peaceful. Bring us back, Lord, to You, and we will repent; renew our days as of old.

67 Pis-chu li

פתחו לי

Pis-chu li sha-aray tzedek,
ovŏ vom ŏdeh koh. Zeh
hasha-ar lashem tzadikim
yovŏ-u vŏ.

פִּתְחוּ לִי שַׁעֲרֵי צֶדֶק,
אָבֹא בָם אוֹדֶה קָהּ. זֶה
הַשַּׁעַר לַה' צַדִּיקִים
יָבֹאוּ בוֹ.

Open the gates of righteousness for me; I will go in and praise God. This is the gateway to the Lord through which the righteous may enter.

68 Tzavayh

צוה

Tzavayh y'shu-ŏs ya-akŏv.

צַוֵּה יְשׁוּעוֹת יַעֲקֹב.

Give a command for the salvation of Jacob.

69 Tziyŏn

ציון

Tziyŏn halŏ tish-ali
lishlŏm asira-yich.

צִיּוֹן הֲלֹא תִשְׁאֲלִי
לִשְׁלוֹם אֲסִירָיִךְ.

O Zion, why are you not concerned with the welfare of your prisoners?

70 Rabŏs machashovŏs

רבות מחשבות

Rabŏs machashovŏs b'lev
ish va-atzas hashem hi
sokum. Atzas hashem l'ŏlom
ta-amŏd, machsh'vŏs libŏ
l'dŏr vodŏr.

רַבּוֹת מַחֲשָׁבוֹת בְּלֶב
אִישׁ וַעֲצַת ה' הִיא
תָקוּם. עֲצַת ה' לְעוֹלָם
תַּעֲמֹד, מַחְשְׁבוֹת לִבּוֹ
לְדֹר וָדֹר.

Many ideas pass through a man's heart, but the Lord's plan will endure. The Lord's plan stands firm forever; His ideas through all generations.

71 S'u sh'orim

שאו שערים

S'u sh'orim roshaychem
v'hinosu pis-chay ŏlom,
v'yovŏ melech hakovŏd.

שְׂאוּ שְׁעָרִים רָאשֵׁיכֶם
וְהִנָּשְׂאוּ פִּתְחֵי עוֹלָם,
וְיָבוֹא מֶלֶךְ הַכָּבוֹד.

Hold up your heads, gates; raise yourselves, everlasting doors; let the King of glory enter.

72 Shabchi y'rushola-yim

Shabchi y'rushola-yim es hashem,
hal'li elōka-yich tziyōn.

שבחי ירושלים

שַׁבְּחִי יְרוּשָׁלַיִם אֶת־ה',
הַלְלִי אֱלֹקַיִךְ צִיּוֹן.

Glorify the Lord, Jerusalem; praise your God, Zion.

73 Shiroh chadoshoh

Shiroh chadoshoh shibchu
g'ulim l'shimcho al s'fas
ha-yom. Yachad kulom hōdu
v'himlichu v'omru: hashem
yimlōch l'ōlam vo-ed.

שירה חדשה

שִׁירָה חֲדָשָׁה שִׁבְּחוּ
גְאוּלִים לְשִׁמְךָ עַל שְׁפַת
הַיָּם. יַחַד כֻּלָּם הוֹדוּ
וְהִמְלִיכוּ וְאָמְרוּ: ה'
יִמְלֹךְ לְעוֹלָם וָעֶד.

The redeemed people sang a new song of praise to Your name at the sea shore. Together they all gave thanks and proclaimed Your sovreignty, saying: The Lord will reign forever.

74 Sh'ma b'ni

Sh'ma b'ni musar ovicho
v'al titōsh tōras imecho.

שמע בני

שְׁמַע בְּנִי מוּסַר אָבִיךָ
וְאַל תִּטֹּשׁ תּוֹרַת אִמֶּךָ.

Listen, my son, to your father's guidance, and do not discard your mother's teaching.

75 Sh'ma yisro-ayl

Sh'ma yisro-ayl hashem elōkaynu
hashem echod.

שמע ישראל

שְׁמַע יִשְׂרָאֵל ה' אֱלֹקֵינוּ
ה' אֶחָד.

Hear, Israel, the Lord is our God, the Lord is one.

76 Shifchi chama-yim

שפכי כמים

Shifchi chama-yim libaych
nōchach p'nay hashem.

שִׁפְכִי כַמַּיִם לִבֵּךְ
נֹכַח פְּנֵי ה'.

Pour out your heart like water in the direction of the Lord's presence.

77 Tōras hashem

תורת ה'

Tōras hashem t'mimoh,
m'shivas nofesh. Aydus hashem
ne-emonoh, machkimas pesi.

תּוֹרַת ה' תְּמִימָה,
מְשִׁיבַת נָפֶשׁ. עֵדוּת ה'
נֶאֱמָנָה, מַחְכִּימַת פֶּתִי.

The Lord's Torah is perfect; it restores the soul. The Lord's testimony is reliable; it makes the simple person wise.

78 Tachas asher kinay

תחת אשר קנא

Tachas asher kinay laylōkov
vai-chapayr al b'nay yisro-ayl.

תַּחַת אֲשֶׁר קִנֵּא לֵאלֹקָיו
וַיְכַפֵּר עַל בְּנֵי יִשְׂרָאֵל.

Because he was ardent for his God and made atonement for the children of Israel.